Planning to Implement Service Management

Office of Government Commerce

ITIL® Managing IT services

London: TSO

Published by TSO (The Stationery Office and available from:

Online
www.tsoshop.co.uk

Mail, Telephone, Fax & E-mail
TSO
PO Box 29, Norwich, NR3 1GN
Telephone orders/General enquiries: 0870 600 5522
Fax orders: 0870 600 5533
E-mail: customer.services@tso.co.uk
Textphone 0870 240 3701

TSO Shops
123 Kingsway, London, WC2B 6PQ
020 7242 6393 Fax 020 7242 6394
68-69 Bull Street, Birmingham B4 6AD
0121 236 9696 Fax 0121 236 9699
9-21 Princess Street, Manchester M60 8AS
0161 834 7201 Fax 0161 833 0634
16 Arthur Street, Belfast BT1 4GD
028 9023 8451 Fax 028 9023 5401
18-19 High Street, Cardiff CF10 1PT
029 2039 5548 Fax 029 2038 4347
71 Lothian Road, Edinburgh EH3 9AZ
0870 606 5566 Fax 0870 606 5588

TSO Accredited Agents
(see Yellow Pages)

and through good booksellers

For further information on OGC products, contact:

OGC Service Desk
Rosebery Court
St Andrews Business Park
Norwich NR7 0HS
Telephone +44 (0) 845 000 4999

First published 2002
Sixth impression 2006

ISBN 0 11 330877 9

Printed in the United Kingdom for The Stationery Office.
ID186819   c30   04/06

Titles within the ITIL series include:

Service Support (Published 2000)
Service Desk and the Process of Incident
Management, Problem Management, Configuration
Management, Change Management and
Release Management   ISBN 0 11 330015 8

Service Delivery (Published 2001)
Capacity Management, Availability Management,
Service Level Management, IT Service Continuity,
Financial Management for IT Services and
Customer Relationship Management   ISBN 0 11 330017 4

ICT Infrastructure Management (Published 2002)   ISBN 0 11 330865 5
Application Management (Published 2002)   ISBN 0 11 330866 3
Security Management   ISBN 0 11 330014 X
Business Perspective: The IS View on Delivering Services to the Business ISBN 0 11 330894 9

ITIL back catalogue – an historical repository available as PDF downloads from www.tso.co.uk/ITIL

The managers' set
The complementary guidance set
Environmental management, strategy and computer operations set

CONTENTS

x

FOREWORD

Organisations are increasingly dependent on electronic delivery of services to meet Customer needs. This means a requirement for high quality IT services, matched to business needs and User requirements as they evolve.

OGC's ITIL (IT Infrastructure Library) is the most widely accepted approach to IT Service Management in the world. ITIL provides a cohesive set of best practice, drawn from the public and private sectors internationally, supported by a comprehensive qualification scheme, accredited training organisations, implementation and assessment tools.

Bob Assirati

OGC

The ethos behind the development of ITIL (IT Infrastructure Library) is the recognition that organisations are increasingly dependent upon IT to satisfy their corporate aims and meet their business needs. This growing dependency leads to growing needs for quality IT services – quality that is matched to business needs and User requirements as they emerge.

This is true no matter what type or size of organisation, be it national government, a multinational conglomerate, a decentralised office with either a local or centralised IT provision, an outsourced service provider, or a single office environment with one person providing IT support. In each case there is the requirement to provide an economical service that is reliable, consistent and fit for purpose.

IT Service Management is concerned with delivering and supporting IT services that are appropriate to the business requirements of the organisation. ITIL provides a comprehensive, consistent and coherent set of best practices for IT Service Management processes, promoting a quality approach to achieving business effectiveness and efficiency in the use of information systems. ITIL Service Management processes are intended to be implemented so that they underpin but do not dictate the business processes of an organisation. IT service providers will be striving to improve the quality of the service, but at the same time they will be trying to reduce the costs or, at a minimum, maintain costs at the current level.

The best-practice processes promoted in this book both support and are supported by the British Standards Institution's Standard for IT Service Management (BS15000), and the ISO quality standard ISO9000.

The authors

The guidance in this book was distilled from the experience of a range of authors working in the private sector in IT Service Management. The material was written by:

Vernon Lloyd	Fox IT
Louk Peters	PinkRoccade – The Netherlands
Kathryn Rupchock	Microsoft
Paul Wilkinson	PinkRoccade – The Netherlands

with contributions from:

Julius Duijts	PinkRoccade – The Netherlands
Troy DuMoulin	Pink Elephant
Tony Gannon	Fox IT
David Hinley DS	Hinley Associates
David Jones	PinkRoccade – UK
Andy Kirkham	Fox IT
Sacha Levinson	PinkRoccade – The Netherlands
Colin Rudd	itEMS Ltd.
José Stijntjes	PinkRoccade – The Netherlands

The project was managed and coordinated by Hilary Weston of Fox IT.

A wide-ranging national and international Quality Assurance (QA) exercise was carried out by people proposed by OGC and *it*SMF. OGC and Fox IT wish to express their particular appreciation to the following people who spent considerable time and effort (far beyond the call of duty!) on QA of the material:

Bob Armit	ITIL World
Graham Barnett	DMR
Dave Bingham	DMR
Chris Bradbrook-Armit	The Grey Matters
Joel Brenner	Information Security (Canada)
Martin Carr	OGC
Gary Case	PinkRoccade – North America
Kevin E. Ellis BA MBA	Emfisys, Bank of Montreal
Tony Jenkins	Parity Training Ltd
Kari Johnson	
Chris Jones	CPT Global (Australia)
Vladimir Kufner	Hewlett-Packard
Aidan Lawes	*it*SMF
Sue Lumb	NCM Group (Australia)
Tuomas Nurmela	Sonera (Finland)
Joe Pearson	Icon (South Africa)
Rene Posthumus	Ultracomp B.V.
Capt. Steve Tremblay	Department of National Defence, Canada
Bridget Veitch	Xansa
Bas Verest	CMG – The Netherlands
Guus Welter	Interpay (The Netherlands)
David Wheeldon	CEC Europe
Abbey Wiltse	HP Canada

Contact information

Full details of the range of material published under the ITIL banner can be found at www.itil.co.uk.

For further information on this and other OGC products, please visit the OGC website at www.ogc.gov.uk/. Alternatively, please contact:

OGC Service Desk
Rosebery Court
St Andrews Business Park
Norwich
NR7 0HS
United Kingdom
Tel: +44 (0) 845 000 4999
Email: ServiceDesk@ogc.gsi.gov.uk

1 INTRODUCTION

1.1 Aim of this book

The aim of this book is to give the reader key issues to be considered when planning for the implementation of IT Service Management. The book explains the steps required to implement or improve IT service provision.

The book provides guidance on alignment of the business needs to IT. It enables the reader to assess if IT service provision is meeting the requirements of the business. Where the business requirements are not being met it details the steps necessary to ensure the IT service provision does meet the current and future needs of the business.

The aim therefore is to give practical guidance in evaluating the current maturity levels of Service Management and on implementing improvement to the processes. This book is one of a series issued as part of ITIL that documents industry best practice for the support and delivery of IT services. Although this book can be read in isolation, it is recommended that it be used in conjunction with the other ITIL books. Service Management is a generic concept and the guidance in the ITIL books is applicable generically. The guidance is also scaleable – applicable to both small and large organisations. It applies to distributed and centralised systems, whether in-house or supplied by third parties. It is neither bureaucratic nor unwieldy if implemented sensibly and in full recognition of the business needs of the organisation.

1.2 Scope of this book

This book focuses on the Planning for Implementation of the core Service Management processes, but the concepts are generally applicable for all the other ITIL disciplines.

1.2.1 Target audience

This book is relevant to anyone involved in the delivery or support of IT services. It is particularly relevant to anyone who wants to review the current IT Service Management practices within an organisation to understand where there are weaknesses and to identify the strengths. When these have been identified, implementing a Continuous Service Improvement Programme (CSIP) is the best way to build on the strengths and address the weaknesses. A CSIP is likely to become a major programme of work, which may be composed of many separate but related Projects – the OGC publication *Managing Successful Programmes* gives detailed guidance on a formal approach to Programme Management. It is applicable to anyone involved in the management or day-to-day practice of Service Management. Read the *Service Delivery* and *Service Support* books to understand the Service Management processes and read this book to understand how to plan for and implement the processes – the *Service Delivery* and *Service Support* set or this book can be read first.

There are several ways of delivering an IT service, such as in-house, outsourced and partnership. Even though this book is written mainly from an in-house service provider's perspective it is generally relevant to all other methods of service provision. So those involved in outsourced service provision or working in partnerships will find that most of this book is applicable to them. Business managers will find the book helpful in understanding and establishing best practice IT services and support. Managers from supplier organisations will also find this book relevant when setting up agreements for the delivery and support of services.

1.3   ITIL (IT Infrastructure Library)

Developed from the late 1980s, ITIL has become the worldwide *de facto* standard in Service Management. Starting as a guide for UK government, the framework has proved to be useful to organisations in all sectors through its adoption by many Service Management companies as the basis for consultancy, education and software tools support. Today, ITIL is known and used worldwide.

The reasons for its success are explained in the remainder of this Section:

1.3.1   Deleted

1.3.2   Best practice framework

ITIL documents industry best practice guidance. It has proved its value from the very beginning. Initially, OGC collected information on how various organisations addressed Service Management, analysed this and filtered those issues that would prove useful to OGC and to its Customers in UK central government. Other organisations found that the guidance was generally applicable and markets outside of government were very soon created by the service industry.

Being a framework, ITIL describes the contours of organising Service Management. The models show the goals, general activities, inputs and outputs of the various processes, which can be incorporated within IT organisations. ITIL does not cast in stone every action required on a day-to-day basis because that is something which will differ from organisation to organisation. Instead it focuses on best practice that can be utilised in different ways according to need. Figure 1.1 shows the scope of the library with the *Service Delivery* and *Service Support* books focusing on the processes of IT Service Management.

Thanks to this framework of proven best practice, ITIL can be used within organisations with existing methods and activities in Service Management. Using ITIL does not imply a completely new way of thinking and acting. It provides a framework in which to place existing methods and activities in a structured context. By emphasising the relationships between the processes, any lack of communication and cooperation between various IT functions can be eliminated or minimised.

ITIL provides a proven method for planning common processes, roles and activities with appropriate reference to each other and how the communication lines should function between them.

ITIL books *Service Delivery* and *Service Support* detail industry best practice processes in all aspects of Service Management. By using lessons learnt in the field this book gives practical guidance on implementing the ITIL approach to Service Management.

1.3.3   *De facto* standard

By the mid-1990s, ITIL was recognised as the world *de facto* standard for Service Management. A major advantage of a generally recognised method is a common language. The books define a large number of terms that, when used correctly, can help people to understand each other within IT organisations. They also help to communicate in terms that the business understands. One common complaint from the business community is that IT staff communicate in technology-speak. ITIL helps remove the barriers and offers a common framework for communicating to the business community.

An important part of ITIL projects is getting people to speak that common language. That is why education is the essential basis of an implementation or improvement programme. Only when the people involved use a common language can a project be successful.

1.3.4   Quality approach and standards

In the past, many IT organisations were internally focused and concentrated on technical issues. These days, businesses have high expectations towards the quality of services and these expectations change with time. This means that for IT organisations to live up to these expectations they need to concentrate on service quality and a more Customer oriented approach. Cost issues are now high on the agenda, as is the development of a more businesslike attitude to provision of service.

ITIL focuses on providing high quality services with a particular focus on Customer relationships. This means that the IT organisation should provide whatever is agreed with Customers, which implies a strong relationship between the IT organisation and their Customers and partners.

Tactical processes are centred on the relationships between the IT organisation and their Customers. Service Delivery is partially concerned with setting up agreements and monitoring the targets within these agreements. Meanwhile, on the operational level, the Service Support processes can be viewed as delivering services as laid down in these agreements. On both levels there is a strong relationship with quality systems such as ISO 9000 and a total quality framework such as European Framework for Quality Management (EFQM). ITIL supports these quality systems by providing defined processes and best practice for the management of IT Services, enabling a fast track towards ISO certification. Attaining a quality standard is beneficial for organisations but it has to be recognised that this alone does not guarantee delivery of good service. There would need to be ongoing review of quality of processes aligned with business requirements. There are several Total Quality Management (TQM) approaches to process improvement that are complemented by the use of the ITIL Service Management processes; these include Deming, Juran, Crosby and Six Sigma. A description of these TQM approaches can be found in Appendix I.

The British Standards Institute (BSI) first published *A Code of Practice for IT Service Management* (PD0005) which was based on the principles of ITIL. There is now a standard BS15000. Both BSI and OGC espouse similar, if not identical, principles of best practice for IT Service Management.

1.3.5 *it*SMF

The *it*SMF (IT Service Management Forum) was set up to support and influence the IT Service Management industry. It has, through its very large membership, been influential in promoting industry best practice and driving updates to ITIL.

1.4 The structure of ITIL

The concept of managing IT services for the improvement of business functions is not new; it predates ITIL. The idea of bringing the entire Service Management best practice together under one roof was, however, both radical and new.

Figure 1.1 shows each of the ITIL books with the Service Management processes at the heart of the framework. The Service Management processes are divided into two core areas, Service Delivery and Service Support.

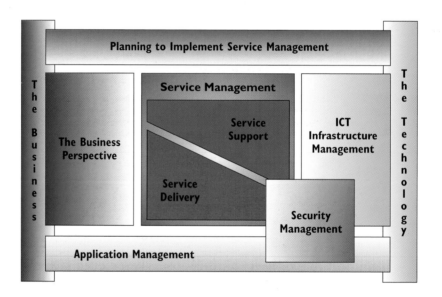

Figure 1.1 – The ITIL publication framework

1.4.1 The Business Perspective

The Business Perspective aims to familiarise business management with the underlying components and architecture design of the Information and Communications Technology (ICT) infrastructure necessary to support their business processes and gain an understanding of Service Management standards and better practice.

The Business Perspective helps the business to understand the benefits of Best Practice in IT Service Management, while at the same time helping the Service Provider to talk on level terms with the business; similarly, the *Planning* book helps Service Providers plan their implementation of Service Management best practice while at the same time helping the business to talk on level terms with the Service Provider.

1.4.2 ICT Infrastructure Management

ICT Infrastructure Management covers all aspects of ICT Infrastructure Management from identification of business requirements through the tendering process, to the testing, installation, deployment and ongoing support and maintenance of the ICT components and IT services. The book describes the major processes involved in the management of all areas and aspects of technology and includes:

- Design and Planning processes
- Deployment processes
- Operations processes
- Technical Support processes.

1.4.3 Applications Management

The book on *Applications Management* embraces the software development lifecycle, expanding the issues touched upon in Software Lifecycle Support and Testing of IT Services. *Applications Management* will expand on the issues of business Change with emphasis on clear requirement definition and implementation of the solution to meet business needs.

1.4.4 Service Support

The ITIL processes covered in the *Service Support* book are depicted in Figure 1.2.

The *Service Support* book describes all the five core ITIL processes, which relate to the provision of the support of services to the User, together with the Service Desk function that draws on all of the other processes. These are all explained in Appendix H1.

1.4.5 Service Delivery

The ITIL processes covered in the *Service Delivery* book are depicted in Figure 1.3.

The *Service Delivery* book describes all the five core ITIL processes, which relate to the provision of the delivery of services to the business. These processes are explained in Appendix H2.

1.5 The objectives of Service Management

The primary objective of Service Management is to ensure that the IT Services are aligned to the business needs. It is imperative that the IT Services underpin the business processes but it is also increasingly important that IT should act as an agent for Change to facilitate business transformation.

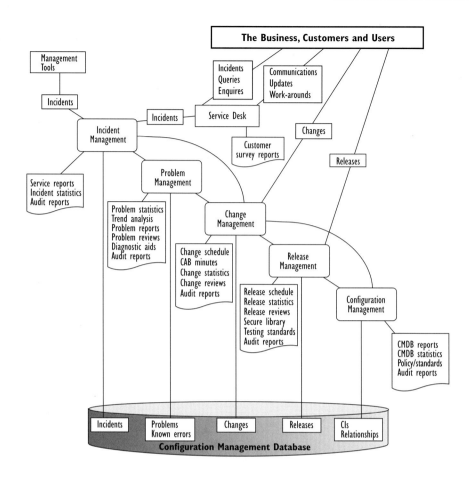

Figure 1.2 – Service Support: coverage

Most organisations that use IT will be dependent on it. If IT processes are not implemented, managed and supported in the appropriate way, the business will probably suffer unacceptable degradation in terms of loss of productive hours, higher costs, loss of revenue or perhaps even business failure, depending upon the criticality of the IT service to the business.

IT service provision, in all organisations, needs to be matched to current and rapidly changing business demands. The objective is to continually improve the quality of service, aligned to the business requirements, cost-effectively. To meet this objective, three areas need to be considered:

1 People with the right skills, appropriate training and the right service culture

2 Effective and efficient Service Management processes

3 Good IT Infrastructure in terms of tools and technology.

These three areas will only facilitate the implementation or realisation of the objectives if they are considered in relation to a conscious, structured mechanism of alignment or 'steering' towards concrete business focused goals. Unless People, Processes and Technology are considered and implemented appropriately within a steering framework, the objectives of Service Management will not be realised. Figure 1.4 shows how these three areas link together.

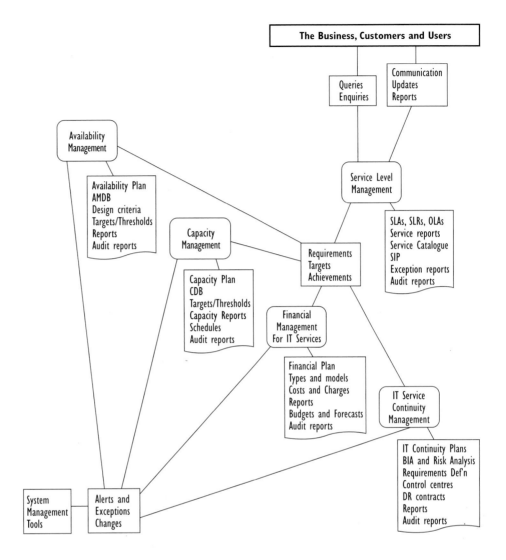

Figure 1.3 – Service Delivery: coverage

1.6   Justification

It is important to make a clear business justification for implementation. What benefits will the business itself get from improved IT Service Management processes?

IT Service Management must make a difference to the whole organisation. It must make the business processes more efficient and more effective. How the business sees IT achieving this also needs to be understood, e.g. business efficiency, cost reduction in IT Service Delivery, increased Customer satisfaction with Service Delivery or more reliable IT Services to support business critical services. In all probability it will be all or most of these things.

As well as considering the current quality of IT services and a possible need to initiate a quality improvement programme, organisations wishing to initiate a CSIP need also to be aware of business and IT market developments and what these mean to their IT organisation. Understanding these general trends in the context of the organisation will help determine how ITIL can best be utilised, not only for improving the quality of existing IT Service Management practices, but also for aligning them with changing business demands.

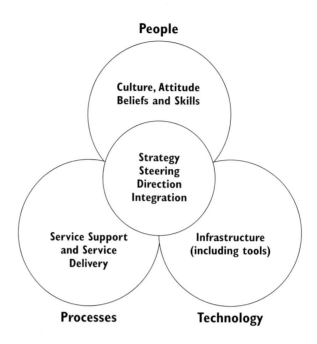

Figure 1.4 – The PPT of Service Management

1.6.1 The business drivers

Businesses are becoming increasingly aware of the importance of IT in not only supporting but also enabling business operations. As an example, the IT world now finds itself confronted with a new challenge: 'the networked economy', in which e-business is driving significant IT investments, and a shift in quality demands.

This means that:

- it is seen as an enabler of business Change and is, therefore, an integral component of the business Change programme
- there is additional focus on the quality of IT in terms of reliability, availability, capacity and security
- IT performance becomes even more visible (e.g. the Internet) – outages and dissatisfaction increasingly become boardroom issues
- IT organisations find themselves more and more in a position where they will have to not only 'realise' but 'manage' business-enabling technology and services that deliver the quality demanded by the business
- IT must start demonstrating value for money
- IT within e-business is not only supporting the primary business processes, but is part of the primary business processes.

1.6.2 The technology drivers

The rapid pace of technology developments is creating a technology push in which IT provides solutions to, and becomes a core component of, almost every area of business operations. This technology push is driving more and more businesses to adopt complex technology to support and enable business operations. This has implications for the IT organisation, which must be able to:

- understand business operations and advise the business on the possibilities and limitations of IT
- accommodate more technology Change, with a reduced cycle time for realising Change
- guarantee existing quality of Service Delivery and Service Support while absorbing more technology
- ensure that quality of delivery and support matches the business use of new technology
- bring escalating costs under control.

It is also important to market the concepts of implementing the ITIL approach of IT Service Management to all members of staff from Senior Executives or Director level to all those who will be affected by the Change, including making a business case for process implementation or improvement. An important part of the business case is likely to be concerned with articulating the problems with the current position and demonstrating the benefits of the new vision. A business case should look at the benefits, disadvantages, costs and risks of the current situation and the future vision. Financial justification for all quality improvement expenditure will have to be made and the business case will need to be approved. The cost of not improving quality will need to be assessed before a decision can be made not to implement the Change. Similarly, cost-saving initiatives have to be assessed to ensure that they do not jeopardise quality.

1.6.3   IT organisation in Change

IT organisations are ramping up their delivery and support capabilities in order to meet the increasing demand for Availability, Capacity, Reliability and Change. However the current role and position of many IT organisations does not meet changing business needs and expectations. Many businesses feel that current IT provision leaves a lot to be desired, and that current IT quality levels and ways of working are not acceptable. This is especially true when IT is fundamental to the business process. In order to support business transformations it is necessary for the IT organisation to undergo a similar transformation process. Often the Change required is revolutionary for IT organisations.

IT organisations are turning to best practice IT management practices, as documented in ITIL, to help them realise their new position for delivering higher quality IT services and at the same time drive down the cost of supporting IT.

1.7   Service Management benefits

The benefits of IT Service Management must be identified in order to justify implementing the processes. The following are some of the generic benefits that will be realised by implementing Service Management within an organisation. They are grouped into financial, employee, innovation and internal, as well as benefits that directly affect the business. In fact, all the improvements must deliver a benefit to the business, if not directly then indirectly, otherwise there will be no business case. Benefits should also be considered for each of the stakeholders.

This is discussed in detail in Sections 2.2 and 3.5. The importance and level of the benefits will vary between organisations. The specific benefits will have to be defined in a way that they can be measured to confirm that they have been realised. Appendix G provides an example cost-benefit analysis for Service Management processes.

1.7.1 Business benefits

- Overall improved quality of business operations by ensuring that IT processes underpin the business processes

- More reliable business support provided by processes such as Incident Management and Change Management as well as the Service Desk

- Customers will know what to expect from IT and what is required of them to ensure this can be delivered

- Increased productivity of business and Customer staff because of more reliable, more available, IT Services

- IT Service Continuity procedures are more focused on the business needs and there will be more confidence in the ability to follow them when required

- Better working relationships between the Customers and the IT service provider

- Enhanced Customer satisfaction as service providers know and deliver what is expected of them.

1.7.2 Financial benefits

- Cost-justified IT infrastructure and IT services

- When implemented, all of the Service Management processes will give long-term financial benefits, for example:

  - by the identification of causes of Incidents recurrence of failures can be prevented

  - the cost of implementing Change will be reduced and the impact on the business will be minimised

  - services will not be over-engineered but they will be designed to meet the required availability targets

  - maintenance contracts for both hardware and software will be cancelled when the components are no longer required

  - 'just in time' Capacity, by providing appropriate capacity just in advance of demand

  - appropriate service continuity expenditure.

1.7.3 Employee benefits

- IT staff will know what is expected of them and they will have the processes and training to ensure that this expectation can be met

- Increased productivity of IT staff

- More motivated staff; improved job satisfaction through better understanding of capability and better management of expectations

■ Improved visibility and reputation of the IT department again leading to more motivated staff.

1.7.4 Innovation benefits

■ Clearer understanding of the requirements of the IT service provision will ensure that IT services are delivered that underpin business processes

■ Better information on current services (and possibly on areas where Changes would bring most benefits)

■ Greater flexibility for the business through improved understanding of IT support

■ Increased flexibility and adaptability is likely to exist within the services

■ Improved ability to recognise changing trends and to adapt quickly to new requirements and market developments ('competitive edge').

1.7.5 Internal benefits

■ Improved metrics and management reporting

■ Better information on current services and on where Changes would bring most benefits

■ Improved communications and inter-team working (both IT and Customer)

■ Clearly defined roles and responsibilities

■ Clearer view of current IT capability

■ Process maturity benefits that are repeatable, consistent and self-improving.

1.8 Service Management costs

There will be costs involved with planning, implementing and running Service Management processes. Costs will occur in several areas such as staff (both permanent and consultancy staff to help with the project), new hardware, new software tools and accommodation. However these costs must be compared with the cost of not implementing suitable processes.

For example, any organisation competing with others must ensure that the quality of their business processes is at least as good as their competition. It is likely that they will not be able to achieve this if the IT Service provision is not of the highest standard. Failure to compete will ultimately mean loss of revenue and potentially the failure of the business.

1.9 Potential Service Management issues

There will be difficulties with planning, implementing and running the IT Service Management processes. Most, if not all, organisations will encounter one or more of the issues detailed in the table below. More often than not issues impact the ultimate results and realisation of perceived benefits. It is important that this is recognised from the outset. Consider similar large Change Programmes in organisations; have these been implemented without any issues arising? As can be seen from Table 1.1, there is a daunting list of issues that can be overlooked or inadequately addressed:

Issue	How to avoid
An overall lack of commitment from IT staff and Customers	Conduct awareness campaigns to provide general information and clearly publicise the business and personal benefits that will be realised by implementing Service Management. Also involve as many people as possible in the decision-making process to gain their commitment.
Insufficient commitment/interest from senior business management Commitment is more than making funds or resources available	Conduct awareness campaigns for IT Customers stressing the financial and business benefits.
Insufficient knowledge of business strategy	Arrange strategy workshops with senior business and IT decision makers, and develop better working relationships between the business and IT.
Resistance to Change	Raise awareness of the benefits and involve existing staff in designing new processes and procedures.
How to maintain 'business as usual' while implementing Change with limited resources	Release staff on a full or part time basis to work on the CSIP by bringing in temporary staff to 'back fill' the permanent positions. This is often preferable to bringing in temporary staff to concentrate on the new programme of work.
Lack of planning	All quality improvement initiatives should be implemented by the use of a structured Project Management method such as PRINCE2 to ensure appropriate planning is undertaken.
Inappropriate expenditure: too little and the processes will not be implemented and run effectively, too much and the cost justification will be lost	Ensure that all expenditure is cost justified from the business perspective and that funds are allocated.
Lack of staff skill	It is vitally important that the concepts of ITIL are well known and understood. ITIL foundation and management training is now widely available leading to an internationally recognised qualification developed by the ISEB and EXIN examination boards. Ensure that everyone has the appropriate skills for the job and have received the correct amount of training. In addition it would be beneficial for IT staff to receive business-related training covering the broader aspects of IT Infrastructure. Far too often IT is accused of not knowing enough about the business and its needs.

Lack of (or inadequate) tools to underpin the defined processes	Appropriate tool selection should be made with the use of products that underpin the defined processes not dictate the processes.
Lack of service culture	Ensure that everyone recognises the Customer (could be internal or external) and realises that they are delivering service. Leading by example to ensure a shift to a Customer focus attitude that must be re-emphasised regularly.
Not knowing where to start	Assess the areas of greatest need by performing an assessment of the current situation. Set up a project which includes short, medium and long-term initiatives.
Making the business case	All Service and Quality improvement initiatives must ultimately show benefits to the business (if they do not show these benefits, do not do it!); these should be assessed and documented.
Staff not given sufficient authority to make the required decisions	It is important that staff are given the appropriate empowerment to enable the processes they are planning, implementing or running to be as efficient and effective as possible. Also give good reasons in feedback when requests are discounted.
Loss of the Service Management 'champion' (the person driving the implementation)	Do not expect one person to do too much and do not leave all initiatives with one person. Ensure that there is a team (maybe part time) of people, who can champion the improvement, involved in the CSIPs.
Loss of impetus during the implementation project	Ensure that staff are given sufficient time to do the job and that there are sufficient people involved in the project.
Difficulties seeing the overall picture resulting in over-focus on isolated or unconnected processes	Ensure the programme of work is set up with high-level objectives as well as detailed low-level objectives. Ensure that some emphasis is placed on the end-to-end process. Also that the processes are at least interfaced and at best integrated with each other.
No-one accountable	Someone should be given the task of managing the overall implementation and this person should be held responsible. Ideally this is not the person who is actually doing the work on a day-to-day basis.
Failing to quantify and specify the desired results and benefits as they relate to the organisation's situation and drivers or a failure to capture, measure and report on results and benefits	Consult key stakeholders (including Customers and Users of the IT services) in quantifying and specifying the desired results and benefits and then ensure they are measured and reported on.

Issue	How to avoid
Expecting major benefits too quickly	To maintain enthusiasm and commitment quick wins must also be realised and expectations managed as to when longer-term results and benefits will be realised.
Not understanding that the desired results and benefits can only be obtained by the implementation and integration of a number of ITIL processes	Ensure an overall process is designed combining the individual ITIL processes.
Not understanding that implementing Service Management to achieve results and benefits is a combination of people, process, and technology	Ensure that processes are defined with people in mind to implement and run them. Integrated solution, using the appropriate technology, supporting both the processes and the people.
Handover from development to live operation is not handled effectively	The Transfer To Operation (TTO) must be planned for as well. Ideally some members of the project team will be involved in the ongoing operation. It is vitally important that all supporting documentation is produced.
Failure to Implement and Deliver	Be realistic in the estimation of resources and the setting of timelines. Break projects into smaller, more manageable pieces.

Table 1.1 – Potential Service Management issues

These issues are discussed in more detail throughout the book.

1.9.1   Management commitment

Management commitment is about motivating and leading by example. If Management does not support the use of best practice openly and demonstrably, or is not fully committed to Change and innovation, then staff cannot be expected to improve themselves, Service Management processes or service to Customers. Genuine Management commitment is absolutely essential to 'staying the course' when implementing or improving Service Management in an organisation.

1.10   Service Management processes

1.10.1   The processes

All the processes described in ITIL relate to each other. Of the Service Management set, half are detailed in the Service Delivery book and half in the book on Service Support. These processes are explained in Appendix H.

1.10.2 Which to implement first

The question often asked is, 'Which process shall I implement first?' The real answer is, all of them, as the true value of implementing all of the Service Management processes is far greater than the sum of the individual processes. All the processes interrelate with the other processes and in some cases are totally dependent on others. Alternative approaches are explored in Appendix E. However:

- it is not practical to implement a Configuration Management Database (CMDB) without Change Management – the data would quickly become out of date as uncontrolled Changes were implemented

- it is not appropriate to charge for IT service provision as part of an overall Financial Management process without having Service Level Agreements in place defining what services are being delivered for these charges

- it is impossible to perform the activities of Problem Management unless accurate and complete Incident data is recorded as part of the Incident Management process.

While recognising that, to get the complete benefit of implementing IT Service Management, all of the processes need to be addressed, it is also recognised that it is unlikely that organisations can do everything at once. It is therefore recommended that the areas of greatest needs be addressed first. A detailed assessment needs to be undertaken to ascertain the strengths and weaknesses of the IT service provision. This should be undertaken by performing Customer satisfaction surveys, by talking to Customers, by talking to IT staff and by analysing the processes in action. From this assessment, short, medium and long-term strategies can be developed. It may be that 'quick wins' will need to be implemented in the short term to improve the current situation but these improved processes may have to be discarded or amended as part of the medium or long-term strategies. If 'quick wins' are implemented it is important that they are not done at the expense of the long-term objectives so these must be considered at all times. However, every organisation will have to start somewhere and the starting point will be wherever the organisation is now in terms of IT Service Management maturity. Implementation priorities should be set against the goals of a CSIP. For example, if availability of IT services is a critical issue focus on those processes aimed at maximising availability (e.g. Incident Management, Problem Management, Change Management and Availability Management). Throughout the implementation process key players must be involved in the decision-making process. These will include receivers as well as providers of the service. There can be a tendency when analysing the areas of greatest need to go straight for tools to improve the situation. Workshops or focus groups will be beneficial in understanding the requirements and the most suitable process for implementation that will include People, Processes and Technology within the Steering framework outlined in Figure 1.4.

Full details of implementation priorities are given in Chapter 4.

Figure 1.5 illustrates the overall approach that should be taken to improve the quality of service provision. It is important that when implementing or improving Service Management processes a structured Project Management method such as PRINCE2 is used. The improvement process can be summarised as firstly understanding the vision by ascertaining the high-level business objectives. The 'vision setting' should set and align business and IT strategies. Secondly, assessing the current situation to identify strengths that can be built on and weaknesses that need to be addressed. So, 'Where are we now?' is an analysis of the current position in terms of the business, organisation, people, and process. Thirdly, 'Where do we want to be?' is a development of the principles defined in the vision setting agreeing the priorities for improvement, and fourthly detailing the CSIP to achieve higher quality service provision. Next, measurements and metrics need to be put in place to show that the milestones have been achieved and that the business objectives and business priorities have been met. Finally the process should ensure that the momentum for quality improvement is maintained.

The remaining chapters of this book will follow the above process flow, with a concluding Chapter 8 and a Bibliography in Chapter 9. Appendix E outlines a pragmatic approach to IT Service Management implementation and discusses a number of possible starting positions.

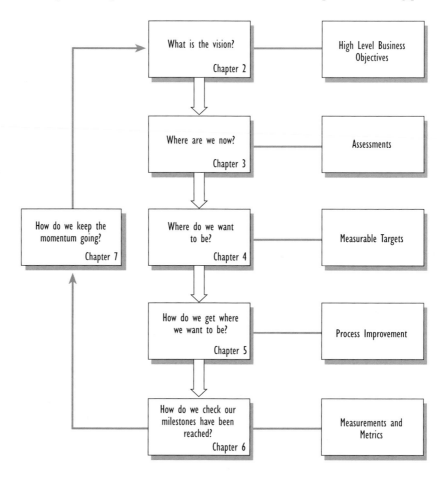

Figure 1.5 – Continuous Service Improvement Programme

2 WHAT IS THE VISION?

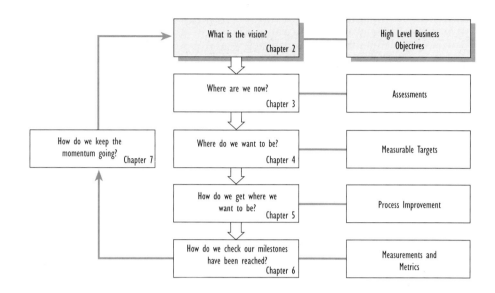

2.1 Creating a Service Management vision

An IT organisation embarking on a CSIP can help position themselves better for success by starting to act like a business, by creating a vision with goals, budgets, and metrics. A Service Management vision is the mutually agreed statement of 'Where do we want to be?' that is formulated by the business and IT together by looking at their forward business objectives. The vision produced should describe the aim and purpose of the CSIP. The vision must touch on all aspects of the programme to include People, Process, and Technology.

A good vision statement can serve four important purposes:

- clarify the direction of the programme
- motivate people to take action in the right direction
- coordinate the actions of many different people
- outline the view of senior management.

Two simple questions that can be asked when forming a vision are:

1 'Can I explain this in 5 minutes to each of the stakeholders?'
2 'Can I answer the question 'What's in it for me?' for each of the stakeholders?'

A sound vision statement is important when forming a business justification for a CSIP – if one is already underway then documenting the vision and aims will ensure that the focus is kept on the specific goals of the programme.

Sometimes it will seem difficult to agree on the vision when there is still significant resistance, or lack of buy-in, from the Customers, or even in some of IT management. To overcome this, it may be necessary to create some quick wins, but all progress should be done in the context of an overall vision (see also Section 5.3 and Appendix E for approaches to quick wins and the order of improving processes).

Example

One IT organisation's vision was to become the preferred supplier of IT services to the business. Underpinning its vision were statements declaring:

'guaranteeing levels of service that match business defined service levels and needs'

'the IT organisation will add value to the business by reducing the time to implement IT Changes and at the same time increase the availability of IT services to the business'

'IT will maintain consistent levels of Customer satisfaction with IT services and will deliver services in line with market costs'

'the IT staff will be professionals certified in IT Service Management and Project Management competencies enabled by state of the art supporting technology'.

2.2 Communicating the vision

Although the vision is a powerful tool in helping guide and coordinate Change, the real power is unleashed when the vision is effectively communicated to the stakeholders. A stakeholder is any individual or group who has an interest, or 'stake,' in the IT service organisation or CSIP. Typically, their interest stems from the fact that they are investing time, energy, attention, money, and/or other resources with the expectation that they will achieve some form of return on their investment.

The sense of urgency ('What if we do nothing?') and the vision ('What's in it for me?') should form the basis of all communication to the stakeholders involved in or impacted by the CSIP. These messages should be aimed at motivating, inspiring and creating the necessary energy and commitment to buy-in to the Change Programme. The question 'What's in it for me?' can be answered by the vision statement example in Section 2.1 for various stakeholders:

Stakeholder	*'What's in it for me?'*
Business sponsors	In line with market costs
	Reduced time to implement new IT
	Increased availability of IT to the business
	Business defined service levels
	Guaranteed levels of service
Customers	Increased availability and reliability of IT to the business
Users	Maintain or improve consistent Customer satisfaction

Employees	Various levels of personal fulfilment
Champions	Improved job satisfaction
	Streamlined processes
	Improved productivity, lessened bureaucracy
Partners	Improved relationships and increased business success
Vendors	Clearer understanding of their position in the business
Suppliers	
Change agents	Fulfilling project work
Trainers	Personal and work recognition, visibility
HR staff	Learning and development
Communication specialists	
Consultants	
Development	Speedier handover process

Table 2.1 – 'What's in it for me?'

It is important to make use of all communications channels to get the messages across. Use the organisation's newsletters, Intranet site, posters, theme and team meetings, and seminars. Aim the communication at the specific needs and wants of each target group. For example, a presentation to computer operators, stressing the benefits of lower management costs, and increased business availability, may be less likely to inspire them than the idea that they will have the chance to gain new skills and opportunities, or that they will be supported by the latest advanced management technology so that they spend less time fire-fighting.

An important aspect of the communication is 'walking the talk' – demonstrating by example. For example, in order to 'maintain consistent levels of Customer satisfaction' it is important to demonstrate, at all levels, that concrete actions are being taken to identify and maintain those levels. In team meetings and communication these issues need to be discussed, priorities and decision-making aligned accordingly, good example behaviour shown and results highlighted and praised. In all interactions in which Customer satisfaction levels have been defined, those involved in, or responsible for, those interactions must 'walk the talk'.

> **Example of what not to do**
>
> At the start of a major CSIP to include awareness campaigns, formal training, workshops, etc., the sponsor was scheduled to introduce the inaugural presentation. At the specified time everyone involved was ready. The sponsor arrived late, muttered some excuses and described, in a five-minute presentation, some bland points on overall quality improvement. He wrote down 3 terms – quality, efficiency and effectiveness – and said that the Project Manager would explain the rest. So much for awareness and 'walk the talk'!

2.3   Empowering others to act on the vision

Establishing the urgency, creating a CSIP project team, creating and communicating a vision are all aimed at creating energy, enthusiasm, buy-in and commitment to make Change happen. Once the energy has been created, it is important to ensure that people are empowered to carry through the vision and make Change happen. One simple test is to ask a representative selection of people having participated in the communications sessions, 'How do you feel about the Changes?' to determine if there is an overall positive feeling or a negative feeling towards the programme.

It is crucial to understand what is meant by empowerment. It is a combination of enabling people and removing barriers. Empowerment means giving people the tools, training and direction and assurance that they will be given clear and unambiguous fixed goals. Once people are empowered, they are accountable. That is why confirming their confidence before going ahead is important.

The following are typical examples of 'enabling' or 'empowering' activities involved in a CSIP.

2.3.1   People

It is important to remove the 'silo' mentality using activities (training etc.) presented to 'individuals' with the intent of overcoming them. One of the most important ways to overcome silos is to develop social binding across teams. Just as planned 'quick wins' are required to be included into projects, it is important to develop a social dynamic that will contribute to information sharing and promote interaction between team members. Planned social activities are a way to achieve this. These need not be complex events. Something as simple as group lunches, or work 'outings' into off-site environments will be very effective. Once individuals get to know each other at a social level, comfort zones increase. So does idea sharing, and common interest in advancing each other's objectives. Other issues to be considered are:

- the need to reward people involved in Service Management, and to ensure that they have a clearly defined career and promotion path
- providing the necessary training for all stakeholders e.g. Service Manager and practitioner training for process owners, ITIL foundation for managers and operational staff
- information and training to Users and Customers in how to interface with the procedures
- hands-on coaching and expertise for process owners
- training that includes not just ITIL competencies but also the softer skills needed such as how to conduct a meeting, how to write reports, how to handle conflict situations
- visible management commitment
- time and resources made available to participate in the CSIP.

2.3.2   Process

It is equally important to ensure that there are:

- clearly defined goals and objectives, so that the procedures and management reports are aimed at specific results

- clearly defined and agreed tasks, responsibility and authority matrices
- employees and process owners allowed to design and define their own process and procedure flows and work instructions – they are not developed by external experts and 'thrown over the wall' like a traditional software development product
- formal project structures with simple lines of communication
- formal User involvement in the definition of escalation and priority codes and procedures
- formal processes for ensuring that multi-discipline teams can work together to develop procedures and working practices
- a framework in which resistance can be made 'open' and 'visible' and can be discussed and acted upon.

2.3.3 Technology

There is also a need for adequate technology support for managing the processes such as Service Desk and Change Management tools.

The people responsible for making the CSIP a success should ask themselves the question 'What do I need to do to enable all involved to make this Change a success?' Another simple test is 'Do you now feel able to carry through the Change?'

The following are types of activities aimed at removing barriers:

- identifying and discussing resistance and proposing activities aimed at minimising resistance
- confronting managers or peers that undercut the Change
- remove confusion and rumours by openly communicating
- confronting people who openly refuse to follow agreed working practices
- involving systems development in developing Change Management practices and procedures to prevent the 'throwing it over the wall' syndrome
- implement evaluation and Change procedures for the ITIL processes and procedures.

2.4 Setting direction

2.4.1 Overview

It is vitally important to ensure alignment of the business and IT strategies. As a result of setting direction for IT, there should be:

- a strategic direction that aligns IT with the business, enabling it to achieve outcomes such as improved service delivery, flexibility to cope with Change, and high-value for expenditures
- policies and standards for consistent approaches to the management of IT
- IT and tool management architectures that supports business objectives.

Senior management sets the strategic direction for the business and its IT as part of business planning, through regular review of the external environment (such as policy initiatives and Changes in the business environment). Key features of the strategic direction include:

■ the ability to exploit opportunities and respond to external Change by taking ongoing strategic decisions

■ a mechanism for accountability

■ a coherent framework for managing risk – whether it is balancing the risks and rewards of a business direction, coping with the uncertainties of project risk or ensuring business continuity

■ a coherent framework for translating strategic intentions into concrete IT goals and measures

■ a coherent framework for translating IT developments into new business opportunities.

Senior management vision and commitment to Change, along with clearly defined goals, are the key drivers of IT process creation. Of all the key success factors in establishing a process orientation for IT, analyst research has identified two as most important:

1 Senior management commitment to Change – necessary to ensure that all of the downstream effects, like work and skills realignment, are understood

2 Clear articulation of goals.

This last point is often lost on process innovators when the initial design is done and the team constructed. Process innovation for IT often starts within a functional area; however, for it to use other external resources effectively, the process sponsor – and by association, the process owner – must have authority over all the affected resources.

IT management should not underestimate the difficulty of getting their enterprises to rethink their work patterns. Best-in-class enterprises invest up to 100 hours of start-up training for process leaders, and typically 40 to 60 hours for process team members, in skills such as teaming, facilitation, meeting, communication and Project Management.

Strategic decisions are not taken in isolation; they are an integrated response to the wider context of the business and its key stakeholders, with a clear understanding of the interdependencies between current and planned Programmes of Change. The strategic direction positions the organisation to achieve its desired outcomes. It is continually updated through strategic management – the continuous setting and maintenance of the organisation's strategic direction, and day-to-day decision-making necessary to deal with changing circumstances and the challenges of the business environment.

2.4.2   Primary activities in direction setting

The following are some key activities involved in setting the overall strategic direction:

■ analysing business needs and how IT can enable these needs to be addressed

■ establishing a policy on Risk Management and ensuring that Risk Management is incorporated into planning and decision-making processes

■ establishing an IT strategy and ensuring that IT is integrated with the business strategy, making business managers aware of the IT contribution towards business outcome

- focusing on the design of policy around outcomes and ensuring the organisation derives the maximum benefit from its investment in IT

- recognising the need for future developments such as e-business and e-commerce.

2.4.3 Key factors for success

The following are key elements for successful alignment of IT with business objectives:

- vision and leadership in setting and maintaining strategic direction, clear goals, and measurement of goal realisation in terms of strategic direction

- acceptance of innovation and new ways of working

- thorough understanding of the business, its stakeholders and its environment

- IT staff understanding the needs of the business

- the business understanding the potential of IT

- information and communication available and accessible to everyone who needs it

- separately allocated time to familiarise with the material

- continuous tracking of technologies to identify opportunities for the business.

24

3 WHERE ARE WE NOW?

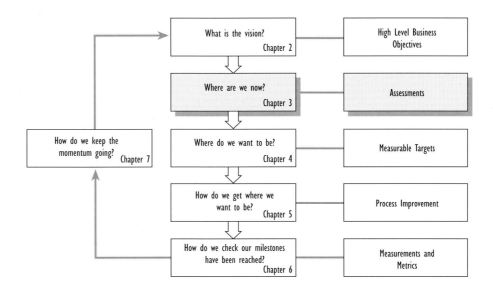

Before embarking upon a Continuous Service Improvement Programme (CSIP) an IT organisation must be able to understand where it is now in the context of a number of perspectives:

- the business driver – does the IT organisation understand the business strategy, direction, the issues facing the business and how they impact IT?

- the technology driver – does the organisation understand technology developments and how these may best be deployed to support the business? Does IT understand how the business views this driver and wants to realise new business benefits offered by technology developments?

- do the business and IT have a shared view of the current role and maturity of IT and the quality of IT Service Delivery as they relate to these drivers?

- does IT have a clear view of the stakeholders of the IT organisation?
    - who are they?
    - what are their demands from IT?
    - are these demands being met?

- does the organisation have a clear answer to the question 'What if we do nothing?'
    - what will be the impact to business operations and strategy realisation?
    - what will be the consequences to the business and to the IT organisation?

Having a clear understanding of where the organisation currently stands will help determine the scale, complexity and effort required to achieve the vision.

KEY MESSAGE

An IT organisation would be wise to have a clear view of both market trends and business developments in relation to IT and not just focus on internal IT matters. An IT manager or IT director who says business and IT alignment is all a hype and too far from practical reality and doesn't take time out from the daily IT management should consider this trend:

'Poor IT performance and lack of business understanding is driving many businesses to consider the outsourcing options'.

Hint

Business recommendation to IT taken from a CAP Gemini Ernst & Young European study (Trends in ICT – 2001)

- improve efficiency of internal processes

- invest in business knowledge

- work on a system to make IT costs visible

- invest in broadening IT staff knowledge

- conduct regular assessments of Customer satisfaction

- continually improve service provision.

3.1   Maturity of IT organisations

When instigating a CSIP, IT organisations must be aware of the maturity or growth stages of IT organisations, and where they, as organisations, currently stand. This may have a significant impact upon the time and effort involved, the approach taken and choices made for a CSIP. (These growth stages are represented in the model in Figure 3.1). It is important to be aware that:

■ each growth stage represents a transformation of the IT organisation, and, as such, will require:

- changes in people (skills and competencies)

- processes (ways of working)

- technology (to support and enable the people and processes)

- steering (the goals and results to be realised)

- attitude (the values and beliefs and the way in which IT behaves toward the business and IT Users)

- a degree of interaction with the business and the stakeholders of the IT organisation

- a need to grow more than two stages in one improvement effort has a considerably higher risk of failure and may have a serious impact on staff motivation and morale and Customer satisfaction

- not all IT organisations need to be at the highest level – the required maturity is dependent upon the business requirements of the role that IT fulfils or needs to fulfil for the business.

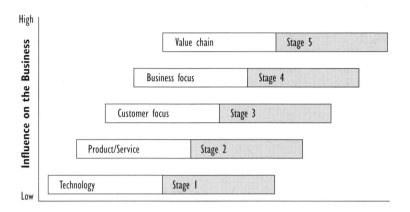

Figure 3.1 – Organisation growth model

Example

Result of interviews with business and IT managers:

Management improvement programmes revealed that the majority of IT organisations are making the transition from growth stage 2 to stage 3 (Product/service focus to Customer focus). This may be confirmed by the popularity and focus within IT organisations on:

- Service Level Management implementations

- Customer care and Customer satisfaction initiatives

- Service Desks.

Business managers declare that stage 4, a more business focused IT delivery, is required. Stage 4 is characterised by 'a deeper understanding of the business', 'proactive advice and good Account Management'. The shift in role required by the IT organisation is principally due to the changing criticality of IT to the business.

3.2   A framework for Change

As already stated, a transition from one growth stage to the next is more than simply implementing or installing ITIL processes and procedures and supporting technology. Each stage requires that a combination of elements be changed in order to realise fully the transformation. These elements may be categorised as:

- vision and strategy – the overall direction as it relates to the role and position of IT within the business

- steering – the objectives and goals of IT in relation to realising the strategy

- processes – the procedures needed to achieve the goals and objectives

- people – the skills and abilities needed to perform the processes

- technology – the supporting infrastructure to enable the processes to be carried out

- culture – the behaviour and attitude required in relation to the role of IT within the business.

3.3 Understanding 'Where are we now?'

Table C.1 in Appendix C can be used to help identify, for each of the elements described in Section 3.2, what the current 'characteristics' are of the IT organisation. This will help identify the difficulty and scope of a CSIP. It will help answer the following:

- How large is the gap between the current role of IT and the required role?

- Is IT steered by goals that reflect business needs? Is there a clear set of goals relating to the CSIP?

- Are the right processes and procedures in place to realise the goals, and the capability to measure and show improvements in delivery?

- Are the desired skill sets and competencies in place that will be needed in relation to
  - the interaction with the business
  - defining a strategic vision
  - planning and steering
  - performing the required process activities?

- Does technology enable performance of processes and delivery of metrics to support the goals?

- Do attitudes and behaviour support a Customer and service-focused approach to delivering IT services?

Analysis against the characteristics in Appendix C will provide a top-level indication of where the organisation believes itself to be and can be used as an instrument for a dialogue with the business. This will help identify how IT perceives its current role and how the business perceives the role.

> **Hint**
>
> **For a more detailed understanding of 'Where are we now?' it is recommended that a Service Management process assessment be carried out. A number are commercially available. A range of self-assessment methods is also available. These types of assessments will help drill down into each ITIL process and related activity sets.**

3.4 Steering IT for stakeholder value

Example

The results of interviews with business and IT managers declared that 'in the future IT will need to be steered on benefits and value to the business in place of costs'.

Findings revealed:

- 60% of IT managers felt that the business did not involve itself enough in IT

- 45% of business managers declared that they did not measure the performance of IT.

Industry findings from various research organisations further revealed a number of other key success factors for Chief Information Officers (CIOs) and leading IT directors:

- CIOs should spend more than 50% of their time outside of the IT organisation. For example, they should spend time in the business or understanding market and technology developments.

- IT organisations need to solicit feedback from all stakeholders. Identify all stakeholders and fully understand their needs – particularly the Customers.

- IT staff perception of service quality and priority improvements are often different from the Customer perception. Yet IT staff sometimes still believe they know best.

To ensure that the business is adequately involved in steering IT and for defining the role of IT in supporting the business, it is important that the IT organisation understands who its stakeholders are, and ensures that they are involved in defining and reviewing IT quality and performance.

3.4.1 Importance of identifying stakeholders

Chapter 2 explains that a stakeholder is any individual or group who has an interest, or 'stake', in the IT service organisation or a CSIP. It is stakeholders who determine when IT is successful and who determine what IT added value is.

Each CSIP has a wide range of stakeholders, whether they are *formally* recognised as stakeholders or not. Each of these groups can have a positive or negative impact on the programme depending on how they are involved in the Change effort. Stakeholders should not only be seen from the perspective of their 'stake' in IT but also from the perspective of their degree of influence, such as 'decision-making capabilities in relation to IT', 'financial control over IT investments', and 'informal influence over the decision-making authorities'.

> **Example**
>
> On several occasions the CSIP failed because the organisation did not complete an initial stakeholder analysis. Frequently the sponsor and the principal roles are identified but not the role of the other 'influencing' stakeholders. For example, in one organisation the directors' secretaries were one of the pilot groups of Users for a new desktop infrastructure and support project. The secretaries as a 'User group' were not adequately involved in an inventory of needs for training and were not adequately supported by the Service Desk. The secretaries complained to their bosses about use of the new desktop functionality and level of support. The business director used this feedback to influence his no-go decision for a wider roll-out.

Sponsorship for any CSIP is needed from decision-making stakeholders and support of any stakeholders that can exercise influence over the decision-makers will help ensure commitment.

There are four key activity areas involved in ensuring stakeholder needs are used to drive a CSIP:

1 Planning
   - definition of stakeholders
   - identifying stakeholders
2 Analysis
   - stakeholder mapping
   - identifying stakeholder needs
3 Action
   - setting goals in relation to stakeholder needs
   - expectation setting
4 Review
   - from goals to questions and metrics.

Planning is covered in Section 3.5, Analysis in Section 3.6, Action in Paragraph 4.3.4 and Review in Paragraph 4.3.6.

3.5 Planning for stakeholder analysis

3.5.1 Definition of key stakeholders

The first step is defining the groups of key stakeholders. Some of the major categories of stakeholders, from the IT organisation's perspective, are shown in Figure 3.2.

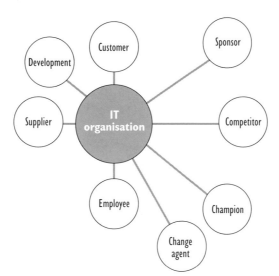

This diagram shows the IT and its stakeholders. It shows that Customers, Software development, Suppliers and Employees are closer to the IT organisation. This is because most effort and attention is generally focused here. When embarking upon an improvement programme other stakeholders come into play or require additional attention, such as Sponsors and Change agents.

Figure 3.2 – Stakeholders

Table 3.1 further describes the stakeholder and their 'stake'.

Stakeholder	Description	Stake
Sponsors	Individuals in leadership roles in an organisation act on behalf of the organisation in allocating resources to the IT organisation or a CSIP. The resources they allocate include money, their own time, energy, reputation and influence, and the time and energy of individuals in the groups they manage. Sponsors could be seen as business board members with IT in their portfolio, or members of the IT or ICT Steering Group (ISG or ICTSG).	Typically look for a return on this investment in terms of increased organisational efficiency or effectiveness or improved financial performance.
Customers	Customers are recipients of the services provided by the IT organisation. IT services are there to support specific business operations of Customer groups.	Commission, pay for and own IT services. They agree to service levels and allocate funding. They expect value for money and consistent delivery against agreements.
Users	Users are the people that use services on a day-to-day basis. They use IT services to support their specific business functionality. They will experience their interaction with the organisation differently as a result of an improvement initiative. Furthermore they are the best positioned to prioritise improvement needs.	Invest energy in using the new procedures and working practices and their expected payoff is an enhanced relationship with the IT organisation and improved perception in service quality to support their individual needs.

Stakeholder	Description	Stake
Employees	Many groups of people throughout an organisation are stakeholders as a result of their role as recipients or targets of a Change. That is, they are asked to undertake the work of shifting their behaviours, attitudes and expectations in order to bring about the desired results of the project. While they may not have a great deal of choice about whether to participate in the CSIP, the level of investment they make can vary from active, enthusiastic support to overt or covert attempts to undermine the project.	Expect to achieve a level of personal, and shared, benefit from their investment.
Champions	Experience has shown that successful CSIPs using ITIL best practice guidance as a reference model are often characterised by the presence of ITIL champions within the organisation. For example, a champion from the User community or the business who will promote the benefits to the rest of the business and User community. It is important to try to identify and form a network of people who will champion the cause within their own organisational domains. These champions form the nucleus of what can be described as a guiding coalition, a powerful set of stakeholders who can be used in effectively communicating Programme aims and benefits.	Key figures that embrace the ITIL concept and work at promoting, convincing, selling, and marketing the framework and its benefits as they relate to the specific organisation.
Change Agents	The individuals and groups who are responsible for facilitating the implementation of a CSIP include such constituencies as IT professionals, trainers, communication specialists, external consultants, human resource professionals, and managers who are charged with developing and executing implementation plans. These individuals are asked to contribute expertise, time, and energy to the project.	Their stake in the process is typically the expectation that their participation will lead to personally important outcomes such as recognition, learning, and/or the chance to work on interesting projects.
Partners/ Suppliers/ Vendors	In many projects, particularly those related to e-commerce initiatives, suppliers and vendors are stakeholders. Their investment in the CSIP can range from active participation in implementing new systems in their own organisations to complying with new procedures.	Their expected payoff is typically a stronger relationship with the organisation leading to increased success for them.

Development	Development is one of the key 'suppliers' to the IT services organisation. Historically IT service organisations and Development organisations have different perceptions about the quality of products handed over and the ease with which the handover occurs. The changing criticality of IT to the majority of businesses means that the traditional quality issues and problems associated with the 'throwing it over the wall' syndrome can, and will, no longer be tolerated. Very often processes implemented within a CSIP will have direct interfaces and relationships with Development and handover processes, for example, Capacity Management, Change Management and Release Management. Maximum business benefits are best achieved by ensuring IT organisations are involved in improving these processes.	Expect a simpler, speedier process of handover and acceptance into operation and increased business satisfaction with new applications.
Competitors	An IT organisation providing services to Customers must also be aware of competitors as stakeholders. To an in-house service organisation this may sound strange. However industry trends clearly show a marked increase in outsourcing IT services. Competitors in the IT services market will offer specific services with guaranteed levels of quality and price. An in-house IT service organisation must understand the services, the level of quality and the costs of the services it provides in relation to outside competition.	Their stake is to try to increase their market share and Customer base. They use economy of scale to be able to offer lower cost services.

Table 3.1 – The stakeholders and their 'stakes'

3.5.2   Identifying key stakeholders

Begin the process of identifying key stakeholders by convening a team of people that have a good insight into the stakeholders and their expectations. This team should include at least:

■ one person who is familiar with the technical aspects of the CSIP

■ one or more people who have a thorough understanding of the internal structure and politics of the organisation

■ one or more individuals who have a clear picture of the organisation's relationships with external constituencies (Customers, suppliers, etc.)

■ the individual who is responsible for heading up the CSIP in the organisation.

The goal is to include the broadest range of perspectives available without gathering a team that is too large to work effectively together.

The team should engage in a discussion designed to identify everyone that will be impacted by the outcome of the CSIP and every group that can contribute to its success. The focus in this phase of 'Where are we now?' should be in understanding how stakeholders currently perceive the IT organisation's role and quality of services.

3.6 Analysis of stakeholder needs

3.6.1 Stakeholder mapping

Once a list of stakeholder constituencies has been defined, it is generally helpful to understand the ways in which they are related to each other from a political perspective. A technique called Stakeholder Mapping®[1] can be used for this purpose.

A Stakeholder Map is a diagram that shows the political relationship of stakeholder individuals and groups to one another, and identifies the Change roles (sponsor, agent, recipient, advocate) that each entity is playing. It can reveal risks such as inadequate sponsorship, poor Change agent positioning, and resistance in critical areas.

One a list of stakeholders has been produced, moving to a map is the next logical step. In addition to providing a clear picture of the organisational terrain that must be navigated to successfully implement the Change, this map can be a critical tool in developing communication and implementation plans to address all key stakeholder groups. An example of a stakeholder map is provided in Appendix K.

3.6.2 Identifying stakeholder needs

Once all stakeholders are identified, those responsible for the CSIP are able to build strategies for communicating with them, anticipating their reactions and ensuring that their expectations are met. By involving stakeholders up front in the Change effort, it is easier to secure buy-in, establish and manage agreed-upon expectations, and gain active support for the Change.

If any groups are excluded from the planning process, and they feel that their expectations are not being met, they can have a major negative impact on the programme. This impact can be unanticipated and potentially devastating when these groups choose to withhold resources, or, worse, act in ways that undermine the programme. For instance, if the organisation implements a Change that primarily affects the interaction between the IT organisation and its User community (such as Service Desk and Change Management), but fails to involve the Users as key stakeholders, they will, potentially, undermine the success of the Change and the buy-in from the User community.

Both the business case, and the goals to be realised, for a CSIP, should relate directly to real stakeholder needs, and not simply the IT perception of those needs. It is particularly important that the IT organisation understands Customer and User needs in relation to IT service provision. These needs should drive the CSIP initiatives and goals.

---

[1] The Stakeholder Mapping process is adapted from the Role Map® Application Tool developed by ODR, Inc.

> **Hint**
>
> **For any CSIP, the IT organisation must take real stakeholder needs into account when determining 'Where are we now?' and 'Where do we want to be?'**

Stakeholder	Positioning	Needs
Sponsor	'Where are we now?'	IT is unable to exploit business opportunities due to legacy infrastructure, cannot handle the required throughput in business transactions, Changes are costly and have a high rate of failure.
	'Where do we want to be?'	Want to be able to realise new business opportunities through the use of the latest infrastructure capabilities to stay competitive – want 'continuity' of operation in systems that affect Customer perception of our service quality.
User	'Where are we now?'	IT systems are often unavailable and have many problems following Changes. Confusion over who to contact and who is responsible.
	'Where do we want to be?'	Want IT to work when they use it and they want somebody to help them when they have difficulties.
Employees	'Where are we now?'	Lack of training opportunities and new value added skills, lack of adequate tool support.
	'Where do we want to be?'	Want good career opportunities, the chance to develop new skills and tools to help manage ever-increasing IT complexity.

Table 3.2 – Sample stakeholder needs

In the examples in Table 3.2 there is a clear indication that 'Where are we now?' does not meet the needs of the stakeholders. There is a need to provide Infrastructure advice and guidance in terms of new IT and how to improve business transaction throughput (Capacity Management). There is a need to ensure successful IT Changes guaranteeing higher availability of solutions (Availability Management, Problem Management and Change Management). Users clearly need more support in using IT (Service Desk), IT employees want more opportunities (ITIL Service Management skills and more process responsibility for 'providing capacity and availability planning and designs'), as well as supporting toolsets to enable them to better manage the increasing complexity of the infrastructure.

Due to the size and complexity of some organisations pursuing a CSIP, the programme may extend over a year or longer. In these situations, there may be turnover experienced within the key stakeholder roles of the programme. If this is the case, the new stakeholder's needs must be assessed in light of the CSIP initiative, especially if the new individual is in a position of influence and decision-making with regards to the programme.

3.6.3 Summary

It is important that those responsible for a CSIP together with the sponsor (business owner of IT or the IT steering group) determine:

- who the priority stakeholders are
- what the priority stakeholder perceptions and needs are
- what the consequences will be in not realising stakeholder needs.

The answers will dictate which benefits and results need to be realised first and where quick wins can be planned for and realised, as well as help manage other stakeholder expectations. These stakeholder needs will need to be translated into goals to be realised within a CSIP.

The IT organisation will benefit by:

- improving the dialogue between the business and IT
- showing that the IT organisation is aware of its external environment and is proactively trying to align itself to changing business demands
- actively involving the business as Customers and Users in defining improvement needs and defining the required role of the IT organisation in supporting or enabling the business
- managing expectations of the various stakeholders
- ensuring that stakeholder needs are prioritised and that the business supports and understands the priorities
- gaining commitment from IT and business so they can and will work together as partners.

3.7 Steering towards value realisation

'Where are we now?' should also take into account the way in which IT goals are set and how IT performance is measured and reported. The majority of IT organisations produce management reports, facts and figures. But there are three key questions to ask:

1 'Who receives existing reports?'
2 'What is done with them?'
3 'To what degree do they support goals?'

The types of reports required depend on the maturity of the organisation. Figure 3.3 illustrates the use of a measurement framework as a solution to these management dilemmas.

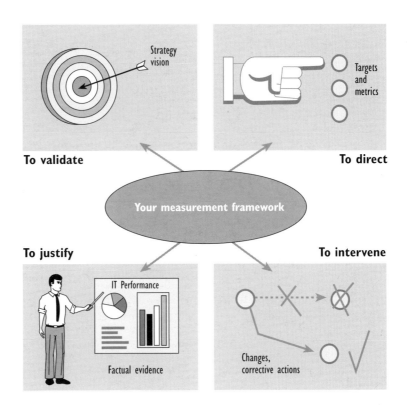

Figure 3.3 – A reporting measurement framework

Example

In one organisation embarking upon a CSIP, a pile of reports was proudly displayed as evidence of 'effective management reports'. A vast array of charts, graphs, percentage figures and impressively rising and falling coloured lines were bundled into thick reports. The IT director was asked if he read them. *'No – they are for the process managers and line managers'*. The process managers were asked the same question. *'No – they are for the directors'*. The initial Key Performance Indicator (KPI) reports had been created by a previous project that had implemented service improvements. The KPI reports were based upon 'examples given in the ITIL books' rather than what was actually needed. Nobody actually owned or used the reports to make any decisions or steer the delivery organisation on realising added value.

Example

In a goal setting management team workshop, involving business sponsors and Customer stakeholders, 'availability' of IT was prioritised as a key goal for improvement. Parallel to this activity, an assessment was conducted into process maturity. The IT organisation considered Availability Management to be their most mature process, displaying impressive reports showing KPI of 99% availability and a consistent achievement of 99% availability of the servers. The previous CSIP had spent considerable effort implementing Availability Management. Investigations revealed that the application availability was poor. Applications were stopped and reloaded throughout the day. Because of poor design, a single failing transaction type meant the whole application had to be reloaded. The response from the Availability Manager was '**What the Users fail to understand is that Availability Management only covers infrastructure components, they are moaning about the application. That's got nothing to do with us.**'

This shows a number of issues:

- the Availability Manager did not understand service quality from an end-User perspective

- the goal and the KPIs did not reflect real stakeholder needs

- Software Development, as a stakeholder, were not involved in previous service improvement initiatives

- the culture of the IT organisation was still very much technology and product-focused.

Although a process approach was taken and ITIL Availability Management training was provided, IT staff did not consider 'service quality' from an end-User perspective.

Simply put, it is important to trace how business needs are translated into IT goals, plans and activities and how reports are produced and fed back to the business. Some key areas to examine are:

- Are there clearly defined IT strategic plans, particularly as they relate to improvements in Service Delivery performance and quality, the flexibility to accommodate Change and value for money?

- Are there documented and communicated SMART (Specific, Measurable, Achievable, Realistic and Time related) goals?

- Are there documented risks and countermeasures defined in relation to non-achievement of goals?

- Are the current IT improvement goals clearly related to these goals and is there evidence of risk mitigation?

- Do current management reports demonstrate achievement or lack of achievement in performance against these goals?

- Are actions taken in relation to non-achievement of goals?

- Is there evidence of communication relating to goal achievement both to internal and external stakeholders?
- Is there ownership of responsibility?

Those responsible for a CSIP will need to determine how well steering is currently achieved and use the results in helping to scope 'Where do we need to be?'

3.8 Benchmarking as a steering instrument

Benchmarking is a management technique to improve performance. It is used to compare performance between different organisations – or different units within a single organisation – undertaking similar processes. Benchmarking is an ongoing method of measuring and improving products, services and practices against the best that can be identified in any industry anywhere. It has been defined as 'the search for industry best practices which lead to superior performance'.

Benchmarking generally falls into four categories:

1 A baseline set at a certain point in time for the same system or department (service targets are a form of benchmark)

2 Comparison to industry norms provided by external organisations

3 Direct comparisons with similar organisations

4 Comparison with other systems or departments within the same company.

Organisations should plan their benchmarking process based on their improvement needs, and should understand that this may require measurement of other companies. Some cross-industry figures may be published by the international research organisations, but will not necessarily include the assumptions and measurements a given organisation needs. A research organisation may, however, be a valuable benchmarking partner, for example, if target companies are competitors.

There is a general expectation that benchmarking is a process of comparing an organisation's performance to industry-standard figures. By extension, having such 'benchmark' figures available is often seen as the first hurdle in a benchmark exercise. However, as this Section will show, benchmarks are only relevant when the comparison is of the same performance measures or indicators, and is with similar organisations in terms of size, industry and geography.

3.8.1 Why is it important?

Organisations have a growing need to get a clear view on their own qualities and performances with regard to their competitors and in the eye of their Customers. It isn't sufficient any more to have self-assessment reports on the status of the IT performance; it is equally important to test and compare it with the view the market has on the performance of the organisation. A positive result of this test and comparison can give a competitive edge to the organisation in the market and gives trust to its Customers. The results of benchmarking and self-assessments lead to identification of gaps in terms of people, process, technology and management. A benchmark can be the catalyst to initiating prioritisation of where to begin formal process improvement. The results of benchmarking must clearly display the gaps, identify the risks of not closing the gaps, facilitate prioritisation of development activities, and facilitate communication of this information.

To summarise, a benchmark is the basis for:

■ profiling quality in the market

■ boosting self-confidence and pride in employees as well as motivating and 'tying' employees to an organisation. This is relevant with today's staff shortages in the IT industry – IT personnel want to work in a highly efficient, 'cutting edge' environment

■ trust from Customers that the organisation is a good IT management service provider.

Optimising service quality is key to all IT organisations to maximise performance and Customer satisfaction and provide value for money. Organisations will be required to focus on end results and service quality, rather than simply on their business activities and processes.

3.8.2   Benefits

Benchmarking often reveals quick wins – opportunities for improvement that are easy and low cost to implement while providing substantial benefits in terms of process effectiveness, cost reduction, or staff synergy. Organisations that use benchmarking successfully report that the costs of benchmarking are clearly repaid through the improvements realised.

Using Benchmark results will help deliver major benefits in:

■ achieving economy in the form of lower prices and higher productivity on the part of the service provider

■ achieving efficiency by comparing the costs of providing IT services and the contribution these services make to the business with what is achieved in other organisations. This helps the organisation to identify areas for improvement

■ achieving effectiveness in terms of actual business objectives realised compared with what was planned.

Benchmarking helps the organisation to focus on strategic planning by identifying the relative effectiveness of IT support for the business. Economy is the easiest area to investigate although efficiency and effectiveness may deliver the most benefit to the business. To obtain the maximum benefit, it is necessary to look at all of these three areas, rather than focusing on one to the exclusion of the others.

3.8.3   Who is involved?

Within an organisation there will be three parties involved in benchmarking:

■ the Customer – that is, the business manager responsible for acquiring IT services to meet business objectives. The Customer's interest in benchmarking would be: 'How can I improve my performance in procuring services and managing service providers, and in supporting the business through IT services?'

■ the User or consumer – that is, anyone who uses IT services to support his or her work. The User's interest in benchmarking would be: 'How can I improve my performance by exploiting IT?'

■ the internal service provider, providing IT services to Users under Service Level Agreements negotiated with and managed by the Customer. The provider's interest in benchmarking would be: 'How can we improve our performance in the delivery of IT services which meet the requirements of our Customers and which are cost-effective and timely?'

There will also be participation from external parties:

- external service providers, providing IT services to Users under contracts and service level agreements negotiated with and managed by the Customer
- members of the public are increasingly becoming direct Users of IT services
- benchmarking partners – that is, other organisations with whom comparisons are made in order to identify the best practices to be adopted for improvements.

3.8.4   What to benchmark

Differences in benchmarks between organisations are normal. All organisations and service-provider infrastructures are unique, and most are continually changing. There are also intangible but influential factors that cannot be measured, such as growth, goodwill, image and culture.

Direct comparison with similar organisations is most effective if there is a sufficiently large group of organisations with similar characteristics. It is important to understand the size and nature of the business area, including the geographical distribution and the extent to which the service is used for business, or time-critical, activities.

The culture of the Customer and User population also has an influence. Many support services are influenced by the extent to which Customers will or will not accept restrictions on what they may do with the technology provided. For example, it is difficult to have good security standards with Users who will not keep their passwords secure, or who load unlicensed or untested software.

Comparison with other groups in the same organisation normally allows a detailed examination of the features being compared, so that it can be established whether or not the comparison is of 'like with like'.

> **Tip**
>
> **When benchmarking one or more of the Service Management processes, the IT organisation has to ascertain which process or processes the organisation should focus on first, if all cannot be implemented simultaneously. Determine which Service Management process or processes to compare. Benchmarking of a Service Management process is used to find out if a process is cost-effective, responsive to the Customer's needs and effective in comparison with other organisations. Some organisations use benchmarking to decide whether they should change their service provider.**

It is essential in planning for Service Management to start with an assessment or review of the relevant Service Management processes. The results of this can provide a baseline for future comparison.

Example

One large company started with the implementation of all Service Management processes. Senior management never answered the question WHY all these processes should be implemented. It sounded like a good thing to do: 'everybody else is doing Service Management so why don't we?'. After two years the whole project had to be stopped because Customers were complaining about poor service. It was decided to restart the Service Management project. This time senior management decided to implement only a part of Service Management (the processes where the 'pain' was most felt) and there was an assessment conducted to provide a baseline of results for future comparison.

3.8.5 How to benchmark

Benchmarking is the first of a logical sequence of stages that an organisation goes through to achieve continuous improvement in its key processes. It involves cooperation with others as benchmarking partners to learn from them where improvements can be made. It will be necessary to:

- ensure senior management support

- take an external view – bring together business intelligence and internal performance to draw conclusions about the way internal resources and processes must be improved to achieve and surpass the performance of others

- compare processes, not outputs – comparisons with organisations in the same sector are unlikely to identify the significant improvements that have been made elsewhere or overturn the conventions of the sector

- involve process owners – their involvement encourages acceptance and buy-in by those who will be affected immediately by the Changes which will be required to improve performance

- set up benchmarking teams – as a benchmarking culture develops, people will apply the method as part of the normal way in which they manage their work

- acquire the skills – people who undertake benchmarking require a small amount of training and guidance; an experienced in-house facilitator or external consultant will probably be required to provide technical assurance and encouragement in the application of the method.

3.8.6 Effective use of benchmarking

Benchmarking techniques can be applied at various levels from relatively straightforward in-house comparisons through to an industry-wide search for best practice. It comprises four basic stages:

1 **Planning – this includes:**

   - select the broad Service Management process or function to benchmark (such as Service Desk) in relation to stakeholder needs

   - within that process, define the activities to be benchmarked (such as incident lifecycle)

- identify the resources required for the study
- confirm the key performance measures or indicators to measure the performance in carrying out the activity
- document the way the activities are currently completed
- draw up a preliminary list of potential benchmarking partners (these may be within the organisation or outside)
- identify possible sources of information and methods of collection to confirm the suitability of potential partners
- agree the plan and its implementation.

2   **Analysis – this includes:**

- collect information to identify the most likely potential benchmarking partner to contact
- confirm the best potential benchmarking partner and make a preliminary assessment of the performance gap
- establish contacts and visits, if appropriate, to validate and substantiate the information
- compare the existing process with that of the benchmarking partner to identify differences and innovations
- agree targets for improvement that are expected as a result of adopting the benchmarking partner's ways of doing things.

3   **Action – this includes:**

- communicate the results of the study throughout the relevant parts of the organisation and to the benchmarking partner
- plan how to achieve the improvements
- implement the improvement plan, monitoring progress and reviewing as necessary.

4   **Review – this includes:**

- review performance when the Changes have been embedded in the organisation
- identify and rectify anything which may have caused the organisation to fall short of its target
- communicate the results of the Changes implemented to the organisation and the benchmarking partner
- consider benchmarking again to continue the improvement process.

Ideally, benchmark reviews should be built into an ongoing Service Management lifecycle so that regularly scheduled reviews or benchmarks are conducted. The formality and rigour with which they are conducted will vary depending on the environment, the rate of business Change, the complexity of the environment, and the elapsed time since the last review. Conducting these reviews regularly provides valuable metrics and trend analysis with which to judge improvements (or lack thereof) and take corrective action as early as possible to maximise performance gains.

Example

In the UK, the Audit Commission is responsible for monitoring and reporting on the activities of the Councils providing local government services in England and Wales. This includes measuring and comparing Councils over all areas of their responsibilities including IT services. A system of 'family groups' has been defined to take account of variations such as types of region (rural/urban), size of population and local economic factors to make the comparisons more meaningful. The Audit Commission have defined and published specific KPIs for IT services, which Councils can submit on a monthly basis to the Commission's database. For an annual fee the Commission will also e-mail detailed comparison information to Councils after each monthly update (with that Council's figures identified while the other entries are anonymous). The Society of Council IT Managers (SOCITM) hosts a website, www.socitm.gov.uk to enable submission of KPIs and general information on overall results.

3.8.7 Comparison with industry norms

ITIL is itself an industry-recognised best practice, which is a growing standard for Service Management worldwide. The *Service Support* and *Service Delivery* publications provide documented guidance on detailed process assessment and benchmarking that can be used as checklists and templates for organisations doing their own service reviews and benchmarks. Additionally, many IT service organisations around the world provide consulting and professional expertise in the process of conducting Service Management benchmarks and assessments to compare the current processes with published best practices and the ITIL recommendations. It may be worthwhile to investigate using these services if the scope of an assessment is very large or complex.

3.9 Service Management process maturity

Figure 3.4 shows an example of a generic management, Process Maturity Framework (PMF) for Service Management, based on the ideas and principles developed in the 1970s by the Harvard Business School and IBM. The framework has also made reference to and uses the labels for the individual levels, from the Capability Maturity Model (CMM®) referred to in Paragraph 3.9.1, but not the underlying structure of CMM. These ideas have been used together with the concepts contained in Sections 3.1 and 3.2.

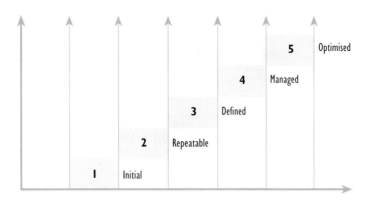

Figure 3.4 – The Process Maturity Framework

The PMF can be used for:

- internal assessment where a benchmark of Service Management process maturity and capability is conducted internally within an organisation

- external assessment where the framework is used by an external third party company to complete a benchmark assessment of an organisation's Service Management process maturity and capability.

The PMF can be used either as a framework to assess the maturity of each of the ten Service Management processes individually, or can be used to measure the maturity of the Service Management processes as a whole. Details of the use and application of the framework are contained in Appendix J.

Process maturity levels can help identify a current baseline of maturity and a set of improvement initiatives. Industry norms are available for benchmarking a wider range of IT practices, for example, the system development processes can be compared with reference material in the field of Software Process Improvement such as CMM, ISO 15504 and COBIT.

CMM and ISO 15504 were originally tuned to software development but are now being adapted to assess a broader range of processes and to define a number of maturity levels for the execution of processes. Indeed, CMM now has specific variants, for example, SW-CMM, SA-CMM etc. that are focused on software engineering and software acquisition respectively. The rest of this Section provides some brief details on CMM, ISO 15504 and COBIT. Fuller details can be found in Appendix I.

3.9.1   CMM

The Capability Maturity Model, developed and maintained by the Software Engineering Institute (SEI), which is part of the Carnegie Mellon University in Pittsburgh, provides an arrangement into five maturity levels for software development: initial, repeatable, defined, managed, and optimising. The CMM enables the software development organisation to consciously choose a certain target level of maturity, and then to work towards that level. The elements associated with each level are explicit.

> **Example**
>
> In the USA, organisations such as the Department of Defense and Boeing require that software suppliers have reached a specified CMM level, or that they can show that they will reach this level within an acceptable period of time. Many software development organisations have therefore started Software Process Improvement (SPI) projects to reach a higher CMM level.

3.9.2   ISO 15504

This standard emerged from a programme of work in the early 1990s entitled 'Software Process Improvement and Capability dEtermination' (SPICE) which is a reference process model for software development. The SEI was one of the organisations to assist in its development, which was initiated in 1992. ISO 15504 is partly based on CMM, but it is less specific in determining the elements that must be worked out for an organisation to reach a certain maturity level. The scope of ISO 15504 is, however, wider than that of CMM, and some aspects have been elaborated in more detail. The process categories have a so-called thematic arrangement (Customer/supplier, engineering, project, organisation, and support). Six maturity levels are distinguished (not performed, informally, planned and tracked, well-defined, quantitatively controlled, and continuously improving). An important difference with CMM is that these levels are applied by process and not to organisations as a whole.

SPICE was an international project initiated to develop the products (process model, procedures, and other documentation) for an ISO standard in 1992. That work was completed essentially by 1995 and it is now embraced in ISO 15504. The ISO standard should be referenced rather than the development project SPICE.

The SPICE framework consists of 35 standard processes that can be grouped into five process categories:

1 Customer-supplier

2 Engineering

3 Project

4 Support

5 Organisation.

The SPICE framework considers five capability levels; these are distinguished by common features and generic processes:

Level 1:   Performed informally

Level 2:   Planned and tracked

Level 3:   Well-defined

Level 4:   Quantitatively controlled

Level 5:   Continuously improving.

3.9.3   COBIT: Control Objectives for Information and Related Technology

COBIT was sponsored by the Information Systems Audit and Control Foundation and is primarily an educational resource for computer auditors. It can be used as a management resource to help understand and manage the risks associated with new technologies. It provides a comprehensive checklist for business process owners. From the business perspective, COBIT recognises 34 high-level control objectives for IT processes. These processes are grouped into four domains: planning and organisation, acquisition and implementation, delivery and support, and monitoring. By addressing these 34 high-level control objectives, the business process owner can be assured that there is an adequate control system for the IT environment.

The COBIT toolset contains both a management awareness diagnostic and an IT control diagnostic to assist in analysing an organisation's IT control environment.

Of particular relevance to the planning and implementation of Service Management Best Practice are the control objectives associated with 'delivery and support'. These include:

- defined Service levels
- management of performance and capacity
- ensuring continuous service
- ensuring systems security
- identifying and attributing costs
- assisting and advising IT Customers
- managing the configuration
- management of Problems and Incidents
- managing facilities and operations.

3.10   Processes

In assessing 'Where are we now?', it is important to determine to what degree a process-based approach is currently in place and supported, as well as to understand the potential resistance that may exist in a silo based organisation such as is described in the first example in Section 3.7. In Figure 3.5, the vertical boxes represent traditional organisational divisions or departments. These are hierarchically steered from management within the department and are very much task focused. The horizontal boxes show the process structure. As can be seen, the processes can cut across, and involve, various organisational divisions. The processes are not hierarchically steered by organisational unit managers, but are steered by process owners. These process owners are often placed within a separate 'Service Management' team or unit.

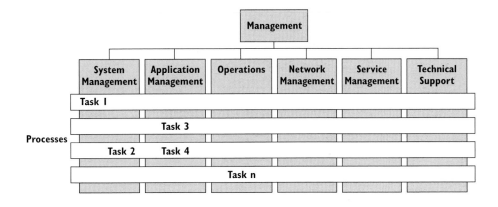

Figure 3.5 – Processes cut across 'silos'

Senior business and IT management involvement and buy-in are necessary for effectively overcoming this silo-based attitude, which has been a key characteristic of IT organisations. As described in Table 3.1, the 'throwing it over the wall' approach will no longer be tolerated as IT becomes increasingly mission critical to business operations.

3.11 People

Very often the only thing standing in the way of a successful outcome to the CSIP is people. In establishing 'Where are we now?' it is important to understand the current ways in which people work together and how their skills and competencies are developed:

- The harder aspects have more to do with systems and structures put in place to support people in their work, for example:
  - clarity in tasks, responsibility and level of authority
  - clarity of objectives and goals
  - meeting and communications structures to support people in the way they interact
  - formalised training and skills, competence development plans and opportunities
- The softer aspects have more to do with the attitude and behaviour of people. A few examples are:
  - the culture of the organisation
  - job satisfaction
  - belief and trust in the leadership within an organisation
  - commitment to the aims and direction
  - rewards and performance measurement systems.

In understanding 'Where are we now?' the following questions will help to identify current practices in how people are organised and supported:

- Do people work in teams to achieve results? CSIP initiatives often require team based working practices. If people are not used to interacting and working in teams this may be a barrier.
- Are there clearly defined job roles including tasks, level of authority and responsibility? If not, resistance to Change may be experienced due to a hesitancy to move toward a formal framework of accountability.
- Do communications methods and structures support people in providing them with clarity and helping them make decisions and carry out their tasks? The execution of ITIL processes requires good communications methods and structures. Very often tools will be used for information and communication between and within process workflows. The use of newsletters, technical notices, e-mails, management reports, presentations, seminars, User group meetings, login and pop-up messages, are all examples of communications structures and methods that support delivery and service improvement. To what degree do they currently occur and how effective are they? These communications methods and structures should also be used to promote the CSIP awareness initiatives.

■ Do meeting structures support people in their work and are the right people invited? CSIPs invariably lead to new meeting formats and attendees. This can be a physical or virtual meeting. Ineffective meeting practices and disciplines may become a barrier to realising service improvements.

■ Are there formalised training plans in place to ensure people develop the right skills and competencies? The skills and training of the staff are essential to the development of effective processes.

■ Are there formal review and performance plans in place to ensure that people have the agreed and appropriate targets set in order to achieve the goals? Good measurement supports a CSIP.

Answering these questions will help identify the gap between current people-focused practices and behaviour and what may be required. Chapter 5 focuses on addressing these issues.

3.12 Culture

Section 3.11 described how the softer aspects of people management and the role they play must also be understood to ensure the success of any CSIP. Culture is continually named as one of the barriers in realising any type of Organisational Change. What is culture? Organisational culture is the whole of the ideas, corporate values, beliefs, practices, and expectations about behaviour and daily customs that are shared by the employees in an organisation. One could say culture is the heart of the matter or a key issue in implementing Service Management. Culture could support an implementation or it could be the bearer of resistance.

When an organisation starts a CSIP, the new organisational structure and technology receives overwhelming attention and almost no attention is paid to the effect on the culture. Culture isn't good or bad – it's just there.

It is important to get an understanding of the type of culture currently existing in the organisation and how this is likely to be affected by any proposed Changes. Conversely, it is equally important to understand the effect current culture may have as a 'barrier' to realising Change. Examples of key questions to be posed to help identify culture are:

■ Do managers display good leadership skills in inspiring and motivating people and do they have a vision of the future and where the IT organisation is heading?

■ Do people have faith and belief in the management?

■ Do people act and behave in the best interests of the Customers that the IT services support? – how often do the words 'Customer' and 'satisfaction' arise in working practices and meetings?

■ Do people feel part of a team; do they work together and support each other and share knowledge and information?

■ What is the current level of satisfaction of IT employees with regard to 'training possibilities' and 'information and support from management'?

■ Are people always moaning about the way that changes are organised and attempted? Do people view change with scepticism and resentment?

■ Do people feel involved in determining the way in which they work and in any recent changes in organisational structure or ways of working?

■ Do people respect working rules and procedures?

The answers to these questions will help to answer the further question 'How will the current culture support IT service delivery during and following a CSIP?' A CSIP will very likely mean:

■ a new set of aims and goals and a change to the way in which people work

■ more team-based working between departments

■ more sharing of information and dialogue between people

■ more focus on Customers and end-User satisfaction

■ more formalisation in working practices and discipline.

When developing and rolling out new IT processes and working practices, understanding 'Where are we now?' will help ensure adequate attention is placed on addressing any possible barriers that may arise as a result of current culture, attitude and behaviour. Chapter 5 addresses these issues in more detail.

3.13   Current tool support

It is important when answering the question 'Where are we now?' that an inventory is carried out of existing toolsets, their usage and their match to the prime areas considered above. Very often a range of tools are available throughout various organisational departments and more often than not:

■ there is little integration or sharing of data between these tools

■ tools in use to support specific processes do not support the functional level required by the CSIP

■ data structure and handling cannot be tailored to record attributes and data to support workflows.

The analysis of the findings should be used as input into 'Where do we want to be?', so that significant gaps can be identified. For example, in Table 3.3, the proposed CSIP may be considering a focus on Configuration Management, Incident Management, Problem Management, Change Management and Capacity Management. Here, a number of tools are in current use. Two separate tools are used for Configuration Management but only one of them supports Change Management. Meanwhile, there are no tools supporting Problem Management while there are two tools supporting Incident Management and Capacity Management.

Process	Configuration Management	Incident Management	Problem Management	Change Management	Capacity Management
Tool A	✓	✓		✓	
Tool B		✓			
Tool C	✓				✓
Tool D					✓

Table 3.3 – Tool inventory

When focusing on the question 'Where do we want to be?', it is important to be able to define specific requirements in terms of technology-enabled processes requiring improvement, for example:

- which processes and functionality can be effectively supported now
- which processes are required and which functionality is demanded for each process
- which data has to be captured to carry out and report upon process performance effectively
- what level of process integration is 'demanded' in the tool support (e.g. the ability to link incidents to problems, the ability to automatically register incidents following 'performance or capacity threshold events').

By gathering and analysing existing tool support, a clearer picture will emerge about:

- whether any of the existing tools meet requirements
- the existing data needed to migrate, if it is necessary to implement a new framework of tools or a new integrated Service Management tool
- where the current skills and expertise in using and configuring tools exist.

These are very simplistic descriptions of some of the issues and the questions that will need to be answered. Chapter 4 describes additional selection criteria and guidance related to Service Management tools.

Service Management tools and their evaluation criteria are covered in detail in Appendix L.

4 WHERE DO WE WANT TO BE?

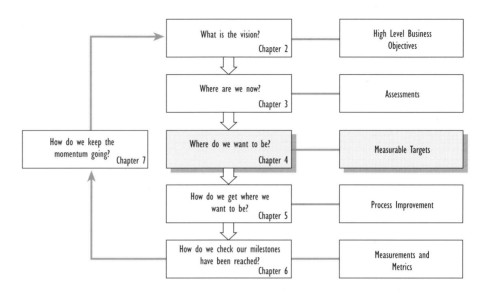

An IT organisation needs to understand the business and technology drivers in relation to its own organisation and determine the type of role that is expected of the IT organisation in relation to the IT Organisation Growth Model. The IT Organisation Role in Table C.1 (in Appendix C) describes some of the key characteristics for each stage of IT organisation growth and can be used to identify the appropriate role characteristics.

It is important that both IT and the business are in agreement as to the role, and the characteristics that are required. The questions to ask are 'Is this a nice-to-have role?', 'Is this a need-to-have role?' and 'What will be the consequences to both the business and the IT organisation if this required role is not realised?'. This helps establish a 'sense of urgency' for any CSIP. Defining this role also helps give shape to the 'vision' of the future of the IT organisation for the business.

Understanding the role that is required will help understand not only the Service Management processes that are necessary, but also the level of Service Management process expertise needed. This means: which process activities and the requisite skills are most likely required to achieve this role and deliver the results and benefits implied by that growth level?

For example:

- At the growth phase of 'Customer Focus' a key requirement is to understand and respond to real Customer needs. One such set of needs will relate to the amount of IT capacity usage, such as amount of mail they want to keep, or the ability to store documents, perhaps even the speed of conducting transactions. To be able to understand and influence these needs the activities related to the ITIL process Capacity Management need to be in place, such as defining workload types and volumes, measuring usage and throughput.

- At the growth phase 'Business Focus' it also means giving more advice and being more proactive to the business. Additional activity sets relating to the Service Management – Capacity Management process will need to be in place such as forecasting growth in business usage of IT, suggesting new technology solutions and 'what if' scenarios, advising on capacity investments to support business growth, sizing new IT solutions and information systems and assessing potential impact on existing infrastructure and services. As can be seen, the higher the growth model demanded, the higher the increase in demand on the activity sets within the Service Management process.

Table 4.1 compares these two aspects. This same exercise can be carried out for each of the ITIL processes.

Growth level	Process	Process expertise
Customer Focus	Capacity Management	Performance measurement
		Workload Management
		Demand Management
		Tuning for performance
Business Focus	Capacity Management	Application sizing
		Modelling
		Capacity Management
		Resource Management (in terms of technology advice)

Table 4.1 – Capacity Management growth phase comparison

4.1　Business case for implementing Service Management

The business case describes the added value of the CSIP for the organisation. To justify implementation, the IT organisation should compare project costs and revenue (savings). The difficulty in doing this, however, is that while the costs are relatively easy to measure (people, tools, etc.), the increase in revenue is more difficult to quantify as a direct result of the CSIP. Appendix G gives examples of cost-benefit analysis.

Results are not always financially quantifiable – process implementation yields higher quality service provision, higher service levels and a more flexible organisation. Sometimes IT organisations find that they are making investments (or incurring costs, depending on the point of view) without clearly knowing the benefit; yet there is no use telling the budget holder that companies sometimes have to take chances if they're going to succeed. The business case should enable the reader to understand the value of investing in CSIP.

Understanding the organisation's target and current situations should form the basis of the business case for a CSIP. A stakeholder assessment and a goal setting exercise will help focus on the results and aims. A business case should be produced and agreed upon, which clearly identifies the:

- role that the business expects of the IT organisation
- current stage of maturity of the IT organisation
- 'sense of urgency' for a CSIP and the risks associated with failure
- benefits of implementing Service Management and the costs of doing nothing

- stakeholders and their expected benefit
- goals to be realised for the business by implementing Service Management processes
- results to be achieved and how these will be recognised
- processes to be implemented to realise these goals in the short term and in the longer term
- impact on the technology to support the implementation
- effort and cost involved in relation to achieving the results
- way in which the benefits outweigh the costs
- impact on the business during implementation (of course these can be positive as well as negative, but they must be clearly understood for business buy-in).

It is important when producing the business case that a senior sponsor is found who supports the improvement initiative and is committed to its success. Without a sponsor there is a high risk that improvements may not be identified and funding is not made available. It is also important that the sponsor defines the basis for acceptance of the business case.

To help support a business case try to gather any existing metrics or evidence that underpin the sense of urgency or the benefits to be realised.

4.2 Identifying and managing risks

The business case describes the added value of the CSIP for the organisation. It puts an investment decision into a strategic context, documenting the business objectives and options.

The development of the business case requires a detailed understanding of the business need and scope before undertaking the change process. The business case should provide senior management with sufficient information to enable them to make decisions about business need and priority of any improvement projects to the business, and assure that the project is justified in terms of acceptable costs, quantified benefits and identified risk.

A structured approach to Risk Management is usually applied during a CSIP or to individual projects. Such an approach would explicitly recognise risk identification, analysis and management phases to ensure that risks are adequately registered, assessed and managed during the course of the programme/project.

However, during the early phases of planning and establishing the business case, it is useful to consider both the inherent and acquired risks that are can be identified. Particular attention should be given to inherent risks in three areas, relating to:

- the business vision
- the existing processes
- the environment and business constraints.

Such inherent risks may be minimised but are unlikely to be entirely avoided and it may be necessary to consider contingency plans and actions to reduce the effects of these risks.

The acquired risks are usually associated with the:

- scope of the CSIP
- project organisation and control

- team capability, experience and support.

Such acquired risks can be more readily minimised or eliminated through management actions.

The simple classification system and treatment of CSIP risks in three categories:

- conceptual – relating to the scope of the CSIP
- technical – relating to the processes and procedures adopted by the organisation
- resource – covering the skills and competencies necessary to deliver a successful Change and improvement in Service Management are addressed within this book.

4.3   Gap assessment report

The results of benchmarking and reviews lead to identification of gaps in terms of people, process and technology issues. A documented gap assessment is the catalyst to prioritising of where to begin formal process improvement. The gap report is used when there is a need to compare data, contrasting one set of numbers or opinions against another, such as current state versus future state, management versus staff, and so on. Gap reports are primarily used when there is a need to present quantitative data.

Categorising of the data facilitates analysis, assists in identifying trends, and divides data results and reporting into more manageable pieces. Assessment reports can often produce vast amounts of data, but the value of that data depends on how it is organised and interpreted; the data can be transformed into information that will help an organisation successfully achieve Change and process improvement. The results must clearly display the gaps, identify the risks of not closing the gaps, facilitate prioritisation of development activities, and facilitate communication of this information.

The success of every IT project relies on a combination of people, process, and technology; the mix of these elements needed for success in a specific project has to be identified by the organisation itself. Therefore understanding the importance of the organisational capabilities or competencies is critical to properly prioritising gaps and identifying areas for development.

Gap analyses identify the risks and development opportunities an organisation has in front of it in preparing itself for successful IT implementation. If all processes cannot be implemented simultaneously, the organisation has to decide which process(es) will give the greatest business benefit.

Once credibility for the assessment process and gap document data has been established, the results must be articulated in an understandable and actionable manner. The problems should be evident and next steps clearly articulated. A gap analysis summary of results and key priorities should be presented to a cross-functional group of key stakeholders who will be pivotal in furthering the Change. Understanding and buy-in from this group is needed before any action planning can occur. If an organisation does not buy into the diagnosis, then they surely will not buy into the cure. Establishing credibility for the assessment or benchmark and its results are important for fostering buy-in. Discuss the impartiality of the assessment process used, and have information on participant profiles handy, such as number of individuals who took the assessment, number of business units involved, number of participants broken down by job level, and so on.

4.3.1 Example gap analysis

This paragraph gives an example of a gap analysis and how it could be used to evaluate the maturity of a Service Management process and identify areas to address within a CSIP. Table 4.2 details the services of gap analysis from the perspectives of Sponsor and User.

Stakeholder	Perspective	Needs
Sponsor	Where are we now?	Sales staff, advisors and field staff do not have access to relevant up-to-date information or the ability for real-time interaction with shared corporate systems.
	Where do we want to be?	Externally focused staff to be equipped with the latest mobile computing technology and on-line access to corporate systems.
		Availability and reliability of systems used in interaction with external Customers is important in terms of image and Customer satisfaction.
User	Where are we now?	A number of external staff already have mobile facilities. Response is poor, availability is poor, and reliability is weak. Numerous problems have been encountered with upgrades and support is inadequate.
	Where do we want to be?	Reliable functionality, high availability. Consistency in versions to overcome compatibility problems when attempting to share information. A Service Desk that is really a Service Desk not a hindrance desk.

Table 4.2 – Sponsor and User gap analysis of services

Figure 4.1 shows the results of evaluating the Release Management process in the light of these service aspirations. This has been carried out using the maturity levels from the example Service Management Process Maturity Framework introduced in Section 3.9. It shows that the currently identified maturity level of Release Management is level 3 (defined), while the required maturity level (target) is level 4 (managed). Figure 3.4, showing the five levels of the maturity framework, is replicated alongside the Release Management Evaluation Table.

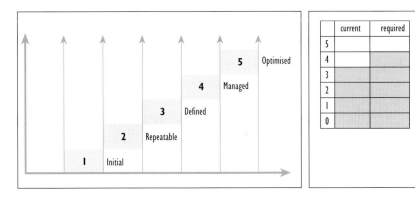

Figure 4.1 – Release Management maturity, current vs. required

The current and required Release Management Process characteristics of the organisation are described in Table 4.3. The characteristics are described in terms of the elements that must be considered in order to fully realise a transformation as discussed in Section 3.2.

Elements to be considered	Level of maturity	
	Current during Defined level	Required for Managed level
Infrastructure components	No clear objectives defined for the controlled release of infrastructure, particularly with reference to desktop and mobile computing.	Clear definition of goals and release policy needed for mobile facilities matched to specific business functions and roles (User profiles). Clear overview of who has which type of mobile functionality and versions. All User profiles share the same versions. Guaranteed levels of service and support to be delivered and integrated into SLM.
Process	Defined processes and procedures in place for updates to corporate systems only in the data centre with some evidence of release schedules.	Well defined processes, procedures and standards, for: − defining User profiles (types of Users and their mobile computing needs) − creating release packages or 'images' (consistent versions of software and configuration parameters matched to a particular User profile) − distribution and configuration are required, supported by reliable up-to-date Configuration Management and Change Management controls.
People	Specialists carry out self-contained roles and responsibilities.	Responsibilities clearly defined in all IT job descriptions covering all release procedures. Training in Release Management practices and principles.
Technology	A number of tools available for distributing software and for building and storing repeatable build images. No central control or defined standards, specialists all have own 'images'.	Centralised control of release packages or 'images' and the ability for central distribution and automating updates.
Culture	Tool and technology based and driven. Little awareness of different types of external workers and their specific functionality and needs.	Service and Customer oriented, full understanding of User and Customer profiles and needs.

Table 4.3 – Release Management maturity, current vs. required

The examples shown have enabled identification of the following key concerns:

- the overall organisation maturity clearly shows a 'technology focused' IT services organisation
- there is a lack of overall awareness of the Customer and User groups and needs
- within the data centre there is a fairly strong process focus, however within the PC support and LAN Management there is a high level of technical expertise and a lack of disciplined focus or process approach
- Configuration Management data is out of date; Change Management practices are not followed
- an upgrade of PC software is a costly exercise because there is no easy way to track down who has what
- inconsistent upgrade practices cause numerous problems resulting in high costs to resolve and revisit for upgrades and 'patches'
- a significant shift in behaviour and attitude is required to become 'Customer' focused and 'process based'
- stronger discipline will become a must in order to support the mobile computing needs to ensure reliability and availability and to guarantee a quality of end User support.

Now that these concerns have been identified they can be used to define 'Where do we want to be?' and to define which areas to address within the CSIP.

4.3.2   Plan for quick wins

Implementing a CSIP can be a lengthy Programme of Change. It is important that during the programme quick wins are identified and attained. The key word here is 'identified', not 'assumed'. Quick wins help to keep a Change effort on track and help keep the energy and commitment levels high.

Quick wins can also be used to:

- help convince Change sceptics of the benefits
- prove early successes, and enable success to build on success
- help retain support of influential stakeholders
- help expand the guiding coalition and get more people on board and committed to the programme help build confidence to tackle even more complex implementation issues and process integration
- help build confidence.

Identify some quick wins for each process and plan these in to the CSIP. It is also important that quick wins are made visible and are communicated to all stakeholders. When communicating the quick wins, it is important to answer the questions 'For whom is it a quick win?' and 'To what degree does it support the overall aims and goals?' and work the answers into the communication.

4.3.3   Best practices for gap reports and results analysis

The following best practices are offered as suggestions to support team members in analysing, prioritising, and presenting assessment result reports:

- analysing
  - maintain the confidentiality of information provided
  - protect the anonymity of all assessment participants
  - analyse results by natural groupings (categories, business units, and so on)
  - start by looking at the summary, or high-level data, and then look at details
  - set criteria for identifying key gaps, and then apply these during the overview of the data – be willing to adjust these criteria if necessary
  - include at least one client representative in the analysis, in order to secure internal support for the findings
  - investigate any data that looks out of the ordinary – do not make assumptions
- prioritising
  - prioritise mission-critical capability gaps first
  - remember that the biggest gap does not always amount to the largest risk for the project
  - prioritise the biggest risk items with the greatest impact highest
  - be sure to prioritise some 'quick wins' as high – these are gaps that can be closed relatively quickly and show tangible benefits, which will spur continual activity through the project
- presenting
  - use charts to present results according to the assessment scale used; begin by showing overall ratings at the top level and then break down charts to the appropriate level of detail
  - always have the original collated results present, in case someone questions the data or wants to see more detail
  - point out organisational strengths in addition to gaps or weaknesses – this information is just as critical to leverage for successful Change
  - engage all relevant constituencies in the presentation.

Prioritising the gaps in capabilities and competencies that an organisation will focus on is crucial for effective planning. Organisations are driven by schedules and budgets that force them to execute the best they can under given conditions. To accomplish this successfully, an organisation should prioritise the capabilities and competencies where gaps exist based on the following criteria:

- importance – how important is this capability or process competency to the overall success of the CSIP?
- exposure – what will be the impact of the risk to the project if this capability or competency is not developed to the recommended level, and what is the probability that the risk will occur? (impact x probability = exposure)
- benefit – how will the CSIP benefit by having this capability or competency further developed?
- effort – what level of effort and resources will it take to develop this capability or competency?

Establishing these values will assist in prioritising which gaps in capabilities and competencies are the most vital to the CSIP.

Presenting to the right audience is of utmost importance. Those individuals present for the report should be key stakeholders who influence the decision-making process; the people involved in the Change, or the implementation activities. These would include, at a minimum, Change sponsors and agents. The way in which data has been analysed, or the Change implementation plans, could result in an audience segmented by department or function.

The means of communicating results will vary from one organisation to another. Understanding what means are most effective to each situation is critical. Some organisations may want to see all of the data, while others may only want to see the summary and to understand the assumptions and decisions behind the recommended priorities identified. Regardless of the reporting preference for detail, there are a few principles that can facilitate successful results reporting:

- Establish credibility for the assessment process and data
- Start with a high-level summary and work down
- Make the data structure clear and easy to navigate (for example, first look at high-level category summaries, then look at the capability and competency details within each of the categories)
- Communicate the criteria for prioritisation (make sure these are approved before moving on)
- Ensure acceptance of the results and prioritisations following the presentation
- Distribute high-level results to all participants as soon as possible – most participants will want to see the fruits of their efforts (an overall summary of results, priorities, and next steps) – showing them how they have been involved in identifying the problem will help them engage in creating a solution.

Where the IT organisation is starting from scratch and there are no processes to benchmark or evaluate to identify existing gaps, one place to start might be Service Level Management in order to identify service level requirements. In this way IT Service requirements can be defined in terms of functionality, quality, costs and time. Care should be taken that they are not defined in a way that results in impractical agreements being made. The targets held in the SLAs will be heavily dependent on the processes to be implemented afterwards, such as Availability Management, Capacity Management, Incident Management, and Change Management.

4.3.4 Action – setting goals in relation to stakeholder needs

As outlined in Paragraph 3.4.1, this is one of the key areas where CSIPs often go wrong – not setting clear goals and success criteria as they relate to the stakeholder needs. Although this is a difficult and time-consuming exercise it is one that helps:

- focus on real results that are measurable and understood by the business and the sponsors for the CSIP
- get buy-in from all management levels and stakeholders
- set priorities to steer CSIP and initiatives
- define procedures, working instructions and reports that underpin the goals
- help identify if desired outcomes of a CSIP have been realised.

In one IT manager's research report it was declared that 'although many managers had a defined IT strategy and goals in more than 50% of the cases there was no way of relating these to business goals and results'. It is important that goals are ultimately SMART (Specific, Measurable, Achievable, Realistic and Time related). There are various methods for setting and measuring goals. One such method is Goals, Questions and Metrics (GQM), which is discussed in Section 4.4. Another framework for producing a balanced set of goals is the Balanced Scorecard (see Paragraph 7.4.6).

The first stage in setting goals is to establish some top-level goals for the Continuous Service Improvement Programme (CSIP).

These top-level goals help focus on results:

- reduced time to realise infrastructure Changes
- increased reliability of the infrastructure in support of key business operations
- increased availability of IT functionality to the key business operations
- increased throughput and performance of business processing through the optimal use of IT
- reduced volume of complaints related to IT functionality support and problem resolution
- reduced business impact of IT outages and User experienced problems
- increased skills and competency levels of IT staff in order to better support business needs and offer a career growth to IT staff.

Conversely, some example goals that do not help focus on results are:

- implement Change Management (Why?)
- more effective and efficient IT Service Delivery (What does effective and efficient mean? How is it measured?)
- higher quality of IT Service Support and Service Delivery (Quality in terms of what?)
- increased Customer satisfaction (Satisfaction with what?)
- reduced Incidents (With what aim?).

4.3.5   Expectation setting

Often CSIP goals are too vague and are not made explicit or measurable.

In this type of organisation, ITIL itself is sometimes blamed. There is a general dissatisfaction with improvements due to wildly differing stakeholder expectations and lack of demonstrable results. Here is a list of complaints from IT organisations in which it was perceived that ITIL added no value:

- 'We started a CSIP based on ITIL more than a year ago but IT Service quality is still poor.'
- 'We have books of ITIL procedures and practices but there is no real improvement.'
- 'We get piles of reports from our ITIL processes that are meaningless to me.'
- 'We have implemented Change Management checklists and procedures, but Changes still take too long.'

What was characteristic in each of these organisations was a clear lack of explicit goals and defined results for the processes.

Example

An investigation into an organisation that had started a CSIP based on ITIL but felt that the promised benefits had not been realised, revealed:

- One of the key issues for the IT director was that Changes never got carried out on time or within budget, and he was getting flak from the business managers. It appeared this was one of his 'implicit' goals for implementing Service Management. One of the CSIP goals was 'to implement effective Change Management'.

- Examination of the Change Management procedures revealed that no additional effort was put in the 'impact assessment phase', or the 'scheduling phase', or the 'evaluation phase', to identify the bottlenecks or improve the planning of Changes. The reports simply confirmed that indeed Changes were not meeting planning requirements. As can be seen, vague goals meant vague procedures and inadequate controls on activities, inadequate reporting and no goal alignment.

4.3.6   Review – from goals to questions and metrics

These top-level goals need to be made concrete during the implementation phase in order to answer the question 'How do we know that we have achieved our goals?'. It is important that a dialogue occurs between the priority stakeholders and the IT organisation in order to ensure that top-level goals are made concrete. Questions to ask might include:

- ■ 'What do we need to ask ourselves to determine if we have achieved these goals?'
- ■ 'What constitutes a success?'
- ■ 'What are the metrics that will support us in determining if the goal has been achieved?'

Example

Goal: 'Reduce the business impact of IT outages and User experienced problems'

Questions:
'Which services impact the business the most? According to whom?'
'What is the current impact of outages to these business services?'
'What are the reasons for these outages?'
'What are the major perceived problems according to Users?'
'How can we reduce the amount and duration of these outages and problems?'
'Where can we book the most success, or quick wins?'

Metrics:
'Current incident volume, outage time and reasons for key IT services outages.'
'Identified 'problems' causing multiple outages.'
'Changes carried out to rectify 'problems.'
'Incident volume/ outage time following Changes.'

It is this information that should be used to drive the CSIP initiatives and the procedures, the activities, the inputs and outputs of the processes to ensure they realise the goals and deliver the necessary metrics.

The example above shows that, in order to provide these metrics, the 'Incident Management', 'Problem Management' and 'Change Management' activities need to be in place to capture and act upon the information and provide underpinning reports.

Additional questions could have been raised with regard to improving resilience to outages, preventing outages from occurring in the first place and automating recovery. These would indicate the need for an Availability Management process.

By using this type of method for establishing goals and metrics an IT organisation can:

- identify which processes would be most beneficial in underpinning and demonstrating goal achievement
- ask probing questions that demand an answer if the goal is to be realised
- provide clearer guidelines and focus for implementing specific activity sets within the processes
- give all involved something concrete to aim at
- help determine quick wins and longer term results.

See Section 6.1 for examples of CSFs and KPIs.

4.4 Goals/Questions/Metrics – GQM

The GQM paradigm was developed in the mid-1980s by Victor Basili at the University of Maryland. The purpose of the GQM paradigm is to help guide individual organisations to focus on their own particular (quantifiable) concerns and expectations. The paradigm facilitates the mapping of such goals to a set of process, resource and product data that can be collected and interpreted with respect to the goals.

The paradigm does not provide a specific set of goals but a general framework for defining goals and refining them into specific quantifiable questions about process and products. The questions form the basis of the specification of the data, which is required to help answer, in a quantitative manner, whether the goals are being attained, and to what degree or level.

In using the GQM paradigm, several levels of refinement may be required to elucidate the goals and the appropriate questions. A goal is normally defined in terms of:

- purpose – this might be to (characterise, evaluate, predict etc.) the (process, product, metric etc.) in order to (understand, assess, manage, learn, improve etc.) IT, for example, the purpose could be to evaluate the Service Support process in order to improve it
- perspective – this might be to examine the (cost, effectiveness, Changes, product measures etc.) from the viewpoint of the (Service Management, User, Customer etc.), for example, examine the cost from the viewpoint of the Customer
- environment – this consists of process factors, problem factors, methods, tools, and constraints etc., for example, the support team are poorly motivated with limited access to training, support tools, and professional development pathways.

To use the paradigm effectively a participative approach with stakeholders is needed. A joint approach facilitates generating suitable questions and defining the measures. Several measures may be required for any one question, but by making the measurement framework explicit the stakeholders can reason about and agree the suitability of the chosen measures.

See Section 6.1 for examples of CSFs and KPIs.

4.5 Tools

Section 3.13 details how to evaluate the suitability of the current tools used to in the Service Management processes. As part of the assessment of 'Where do we want to be?', the requirements for enhancing tools need to be addressed and documented. These requirements will vary depending on the maturity of the process. Appendix L details how to select suitable tools for the organisation.

Section 3.2 identified that Technology is one of the enabling elements in a CSIP. Here, technology means specifically Systems and Service Management toolsets used for both monitoring and controlling the systems and infrastructure components and for managing process-based workflows, such as Incident Management. These issues are elaborated in the ITIL ICT *Infrastructure Management* book.

At first sight, Service Management tools are indispensable. However, good people, good process descriptions, and good procedures and working instructions are the basis for successful Service Management. The need for, and the sophistication of, the tools required will depend on the business need for IT services and, to some extent, the size of the organisation.

In a very small organisation a simple in-house developed database system may be sufficient for logging and controlling Incidents. However, in large organisations, very sophisticated distributed integrated Service Management tools may be required, linking all the processes with Systems Management toolsets. While tools can be important assets, in today's IT-dependent organisations, they are a means, not an end in themselves. When implementing Service Management processes, look at the way current processes work. Each organisation's unique need for management information should always be its starting point. This will help define the specifications for a tool best suited to that organisation.

5 HOW DO WE GET WHERE WE WANT TO BE?

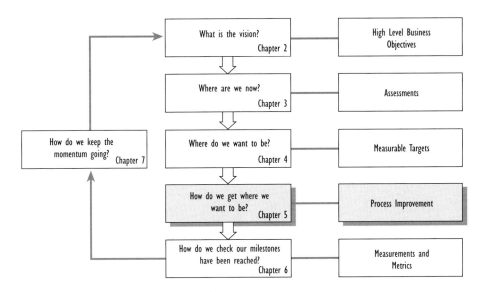

Knowing 'Where are we now?', and 'Where do we want to be?', the next question to address is 'How do we get where we want to be?' Put another way, understanding WHY a Change is required and WHAT Change is required, the next step is to identify HOW that Change is to be achieved. What elements are essential to address in the CSIP?

Many organisations that undertake programmes to improve their core business processes and service delivery capabilities experience the frustration of failure, or only minor successes, instead of reaching their ambitious goals. Many improvement initiatives fail because management do not understand a basic principle – that by implementing processes within traditional hierarchical organisations, they are, in reality, re-engineering and changing a large part of the IT business culture and accountability structure.

Figure 5.1 shows that implementing a process-based improvement programme such as an ITIL-based approach requires an understanding of what processes are and of their relationship to existing organisational structures and ways of working.

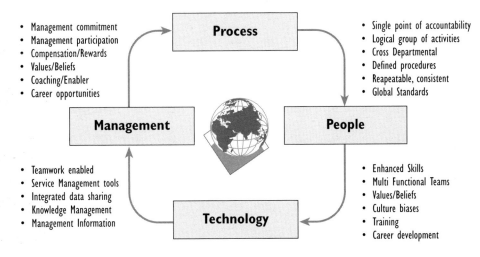

Figure 5.1 – Process re-engineering model

If departments are to work as cross-functional teams instead of systems-based silos, a variety of fundamental changes needs to take place:

- defined and repeatable cross-departmental processes need to be overlaid across silo and systems-based organisational structures

- new areas of accountability and responsibilities need to be defined within job descriptions

- values, beliefs, and corporate cultures need to be changed from unconstructive departmental competition to Customer-focused cooperation

- IT staff working within complex processes need to be provided with more general knowledge; not only the skills required for specialised activities

- a multi-disciplined, integrated toolset to enable data exchange and workflow automation

- management must be committed to Customer focused IT services

- process owners, accountable for cross-departmental processes, must have visible authority in order to manage across multiple silos – this is a marked change from traditional hierarchical managed organisations and may be required to exist side-by-side with the traditional lines of management authority.

Experience has shown that successful Service Management implementations depend more on the 'soft' aspects, like managing an Organisational Change, having awareness campaigns, managing the culture, having good Project Management and training people, than on the 'harder' aspects like the right kind of Service Management tool in use or writing down thick bureaucratic workflow procedures. After all, to implement Service Management is to embark upon an Organisational Change programme and sometimes that Change Programme fails to realise the desired results. It is very tempting to focus only on the Service Management processes and to forget other elements like people, technology and steering. It is also all too easy to underestimate the scale of work required. Support staff, Users and Customers will have to adopt new working practices. Do not expect employees to unquestioningly applaud any Service Management implementation project. Service Management is about their practice and isn't their practice already the best practice? Why should employees adopt new working practices when the current working practices have stood the test of time? Why change old and proven habits?

Implementing a fully functioning operations centre, based on sound Service Management principles, may initially appear costly and bureaucratic. Reading about all the processes and procedures required in a 'best practice' IT environment may result in concern that simple Changes to an IT environment will be very complicated. If Service Management processes are implemented properly, however, bureaucracy can be kept to a minimum and the cost of implementing IT Service Management will be much less than the cost of not doing it.

There are many critical success factors to the successful implementation of IT Service Management. But the major guiding principle is the need to evaluate how the business will benefit from the Change to each process and procedure being considered or implemented. And this evaluation must consider this benefit to the business against the risks associated with failure or non-conformance.

The lack of adequate Change Management in many production environments exists because the need for rapid Change is believed to outweigh the need for managing a stable environment. This tends to change quickly when even minor Changes to the target environment result in significant business downtime.

Processes and procedures should be kept simple and straightforward. Do not over-engineer them; they exist to support a business function, not for their own sake.

> **Hint**
>
> **Many organisations come to the conclusion that a CSIP should start with the Configuration Management process. They identify a very low maturity level for this process and think that Configuration Management alone will provide them with more mature Service Management. So they start identifying and recording all IT CIs, etc. without considering why, and what the added value of this process is to the business.** *Even where this question is properly addressed and results in the decision to start with Configuration Management, it is still of the utmost importance that it should be planned from a business perspective.* **What that means (in this case) is to ensure that the breakdown of the CIs into their various constituent parts is to a level commensurate with the business objectives.**

5.1 Where to start

The answer to the question 'Where should I start?' depends, on the one hand, on the maturity level of the IT organisation (see Chapters 3 and 4) as a whole and the maturity of the individual Service Management processes. On the other hand, where to start depends on the strategic goals of a particular organisation.

> **Hint**
>
> **Many poorly trained ITIL practitioners have fallen into the trap of themselves deciding the order in which Service Management processes should be implemented. This is not correct. It is the organisational needs that steer the prioritisation for the implementation of the Service Management processes based on the strategic goals of the organisation and the short-term gains required.**

Before attempting to identify a process for implementing a CSIP, it is important to understand both the current and desired state of the organisation's Service Management maturity. In order to achieve this understanding both states should be documented and a gap analysis undertaken.

Organisations need to look for improvement in their Service Management processes. Change Management, Configuration Management and Incident Management may be the most beneficial starting points, because the 'pain factor' of these is greatest if they are not working well. With Incident Management, the Service Desk team is able to shorten response and resolution times. With Change Management the duration of Changes can be decreased and the adverse impact of Change reduced. Each improvement of these processes will need a reliable Configuration Management database, managed by a Configuration Management process. See Appendix E for alternative Service Management implementation approaches.

'Where should I start?' is also a matter of priorities. Priorities depend on the interrelationship of the processes as well as the specific strategic goals of the target organisation.

It is important to understand the interrelationships between all of the Service Management processes. This can be achieved by the establishment of a dependency and relationship framework that describes the interdependencies between all processes at both operational and tactical levels. This framework should also include relationships with Customers and vendors.

Generally, organisations will not be able to attain high maturity level with individual Service Management processes without dependent processes being implemented to a similar level. Fuller information on the Relationship between processes can be found in Chapter 2 of the ITIL *Service Support* and *Service Delivery* books.

Example

It is impossible to start with Problem Management when Incident Management is not implemented. Problem Management depends on the monitoring and accurate recording of all Incidents to enable analysis of the underlying cause. However the initial focus could be on Incident Management while at the same time carrying out some of the activities of Problem Management so as to get out of solely 'fire-fighting' mode as soon as possible.

The priorities can be established on the basis of the analysis phase ('Where are we now?'). Prioritising the gaps in the processes and competencies identified in the 'Where do we want to be?' phase is crucial for effective planning. Organisations are driven by schedules and budgets that force them to operate the best they can under given conditions. To accomplish this successfully, an organisation can prioritise improvements in the process or process competencies.

The gap summary of results and key priorities should be presented to a cross-functional group of key stakeholders who will be pivotal in furthering the Change. Understanding and buy-in from this group is needed before any action planning can start. If the management does not accept the diagnosis, then they surely will not accept the cure. Establishing credibility in the assessment or benchmark and its results is important for fostering management support.

Today, some companies offer e-surveys (surveys on the Internet) to scan the Service Management processes so that results can be available very quickly without disrupting the ongoing business and with less effort required on the part of the business.

Discuss with management the impartiality of the assessment process used, and have participant profiles available, such as number of individuals who took the assessment, number of business units involved, number of participants broken down by job level, and so on.

Hint

It is important to ensure that the principal of the Service Management implementation project has sufficient status and leadership to get the support from the people involved in doing the Service Management implementation project. It is also important to present the gap findings to the right audience. Those present for the report should be key stakeholders who influence the decision-making process; the people involved in the Change and the implementation activities. These would include, as a minimum, Change sponsors and agents.

Service Management offers process guidance, not turnkey solutions. This means that out-of-the-box implementations of Service Management simply do not exist. Instead, ITIL provides the IT organisation with a framework, which has to be adapted to work within its needs and priorities. A complete and full implementation of one process can take months or even years to achieve, depending on the current, and sought-after, maturity levels. IT organisations should continue to evolve their processes while maturing, with regular deliverables and benefits. If the evolution process is too long, without delivering benefit, or has insufficient visibility, the stakeholders may withdraw their support.

5.2 Awareness

Raising awareness is an important aspect of 'How do we get where we want to be?', and that means good communication. It is important that stakeholders understand how the business will benefit from a more mature management of IT and why certain changes and measures are being planned. This will help remove barriers to changes in working practices.

In every Service Management implementation project, the proposed results mean that practices and procedures will have to change. These changes are seldom readily accepted and resistance to them is the rule rather than the exception. Changes mean taking measures to manage resistance. These measures cost money and the return on investment is difficult to assess. IT management, employees and Users do not like having their practices, and sometimes privileges, removed, even when they are not really required.

Example

At the start of a major Service Management implementation programme, all IT employees and management were invited to the first awareness presentation. On one side of the room sat the IT employees and on the other side sat the IT management. After a quick introduction it became clear that the management had already identified how the *employees* were expected to change in order to improve the quality of the IT services. After a while it also became clear that there was a deep felt resentment among IT employees because there was no indication of how *IT management* were willing to change. The employees had not received any response or feedback on the way that management was intending to steer and manage the organisation to complement their efforts.

It is necessary to motivate both Users and management to exercise discipline in adhering to all the changes. Professionalism is the key. IT systems often lack control, not for the lack of good procedures but for lack of correct application of those procedures. It all comes down to the attitudes and behaviour of people. Consequently, whenever possible, procedures should be integrated in normal everyday routine, and business and IT should come to recognise IT management as an enabler rather than a barrier.

Some useful pointers to running a successful awareness campaign:

- Full-blown PR campaigns can be used to improve awareness. It may be beneficial to implement an awareness programme designed by a professional PR agency. The most effective way is based on an annual communication plan, in which one aspect is chosen for a period of approximately 2-3 months in order to inform all stakeholders about the background and progress.

■ People tend to see awareness as something that has to be done at the start of a Service Management implementation project. However, it is essential to communicate on a regular basis throughout the CSIP. An awareness campaign must cover the entirety of the project.

■ Make sure that employees appreciate the benefits of mature IT management to their organisation, themselves and their working environment. Any measure or change taken should fit well within the working environment and be within the organisation's capabilities. Furthermore, business Users should be able to participate in the Service Management processes, where possible, e.g. to contribute to self-assessments, to improve on measures and to report any adverse implications on the business.

■ Besides the use of reports, using the corporate magazine to inform employees about mishaps, and the response to them, has proven to be effective.

■ Make clear to everyone that there is a single liaison point to address all problems: the Project Manager.

■ Ensure the procedures are integrated in normal everyday working practice.

■ The message needs to be delivered by the appropriate levels of IT Executive, as identified in the cultural assessment of the organisation.

Example

In one case there was a very tight timetable for the Service Desk implementation project. In an attempt to speed up the development, the ITIL consultant developed the necessary procedures by himself. This was unsuccessful because it failed to take into account the needs of both the organisation and those who would work with the procedures. In order to achieve this, it is essential that those who have to work with the procedures have a hand in their development.

Discipline and an awareness of why the procedures exist are equally essential. Without the latter, the former is impossible to achieve.

Few organisations have the means of enforcing discipline. A sanctions policy can help, but sanctions are not always effective, are difficult and costly to police, and can, in the longer term, be counter-productive. Highlighting weaknesses or imposing sanctions on staff may temporarily alert those who are involved, but the resulting awareness is usually short-lived and will create resentment.

Awareness is more readily influenced by clearly visible supervision (i.e. the Project Manager who has a column in the newsletter of the organisation to address the status of the project, User reports which shows an increase in satisfaction with the IT department) and by applying positive stimuli (i.e. include attendance of IT awareness campaigns and/or ITIL Foundation courses in job profiles).

It is important to draw up a communication plan, which describes how the IT policy will be explained to stakeholders. The communication plan should address:

■ the mission and core message

- target groups
- a communication structure: define who should communicate with whom and about which subjects
- timescales
- methods of communication: i.e. regular newsletters, awareness programs, leaflets, messages when employees log on to their system
- target group identity goals, objectives, benefits, success and failure factors, and possible resistance.

5.3 Managing Organisational Change

Implementing Service Management is to embark upon an Organisational Change programme. Many Organisational Change Programmes fail to achieve the desired results. Implementing Service Management is no different. Successful ITSM requires understanding the way in which work is done and putting in place a Programme of Change within the IT organisation. This type of Change is, by its very nature, prone to difficulties. It involves people and the way they work. People generally do not like to change; the benefits must be explained to everyone to engender their support and to ensure that they break out of old working practices.

Many organisations make the mistake of assuming that solid programme and Project Management structures coupled with adequate ITIL skills and experience will ensure that the Organisational Change is realised. But using Project Management practices is only one side of the 'Managing Organisational Change' competence associated with this type of Change Programme. Project Management structures and frameworks fail to take into account the softer aspects involved in Organisational Change such as 'resistance to Change', 'gaining commitment', 'empowering', 'motivating', 'involving', and 'communicating'. Experience reveals that it is precisely these aspects that prevent many CSIPs from realising their intended aims. The success of a CSIP is dependant on the buy-in of all stakeholders. Gaining their support from the outset, and keeping it, will ensure their participation in the development process and acceptance of the solution. The first five steps in Figure 5.2 identify the basic leadership actions required.

Quote

Prior to the production of this book, a quote from one IT director at an international ITIL conference in response to a question 'What key learning point have you picked up at the conference?':

'Many of the presentations declare that implementing Service Management is a 'people' issue and a 'culture issue' but nobody says how we should address these issues and there isn't much in the ITIL books to help us out'.

Those responsible for managing and steering the Change Programme should consciously address these softer issues. Using an approach such as J.P. Kotter's 'Eight steps to transforming your organisation', coupled with formalised Project Management skills and practices, will significantly increase the chance of success.

John P. Kotter, Professor of Leadership at Harvard Business School, investigated more than 100 companies involved in, or having attempted, a complex Change Programme and identified 'Eight main reasons why transformation efforts fail'. The main eight reasons, which are shown in Figure 5.2, apply equally to IT Service Management implementation programmes.

Steps		
1	Creating a sense of urgency	'... 50% of transformations fail in this phase.' '... without motivation, people won't help and the effort goes nowhere.' '... 75% of a company's management should be convinced of the need ...'
2	Forming a guiding coalition	'... underestimating the difficulties in producing Change ...' '... lack of effective, strong leadership.' '... not a powerful enough guiding coalition ... opposition eventually stops the Change initiative ...'
3	Creating a vision	'... without a sensible vision, a transformation effort can easily dissolve into a list of confusing, incompatible projects that can take the organisation in the wrong direction, or nowhere at all ...' '... an explanation of 5 minutes should obtain a reaction of 'understanding' and 'interest'.'
4	Communicating the vision	'... without credible communication, and a lot of it, the hearts and minds of the troops are never captured.' '... make use of all communications channels.' '... let managers lead by example ...' 'walk the talk'.
5	'Empowering' others to act on the vision	'... structures to underpin the vision ... and removal of barriers to Change.' '... the more people involved, the better the outcome.' '... reward initiatives..'
6	Planning for and creating quick wins	'... real transformation takes time ... without quick wins, too many people give up, or join the ranks of those opposing Change'. '... actively look for performance improvements and establish clear goals ...' '... communicate successes'.
7	Consolidating improvements and producing more Change	'... until Changes sink deeply into the culture new approaches are fragile and subject to regression ...' '... in many cases workers revert to old practice.' '... use credibility of quick wins to tackle even bigger problems'.
8	Institutionalising the Change	'... show how new approaches, behaviour and attitude have helped improve performance.' '... ensure selection and promotion criteria underpin the new approach.'
		Quotes

Figure 5.2 – Eight main reasons why transformation efforts fail

5.3.1   Creating a sense of urgency

Half of all transformations fail to realise their goals due to lack of adequate attention to this step. Not enough people buy in to the fact that Change is a must. Creating a sense of urgency is concerned with answering the question 'What if we do nothing?' Answering this question at all organisational levels will help gain commitment and provide input to a business justification for investing in a CSIP.

Examples of the consequences of doing nothing

- the business will lose money due to outages of crucial IT systems and applications

- the business finds IT costs unacceptable and may insist on staffing reductions as an easy option for reducing costs.

The question 'What if we do nothing?' should be answered from the perspective of different stakeholders, (see Section 3.5). This step could be taken in the form of one-on-one dialogue with stakeholders, workshops and team meetings. The aim is to create a real awareness and commitment that the *status quo* is no longer acceptable.

5.3.2 Forming a guiding coalition

Experience shows a need for assembling a group with sufficient power to lead the Change effort and work together as a team. Power means more than simply formal authority but also experience, respect, trust and credibility. This team is the guiding coalition for the CSIP.

It is important that the team leading the CSIP has a shared understanding of the urgency and what it wants to achieve. A guiding coalition team does not have to be comprised solely of senior managers. A guiding coalition should ensure that the organisation is motivated and inspired to participate. A single ITIL champion cannot achieve success alone. Those initiating a CSIP should try to gain full support from the stakeholders, including the business managers, IT staff and the User community. The team must be prepared to spend time and effort convincing and motivating others to participate.

In the beginning this team will be small and should include an influential business or IT sponsor. As the programme buy-in grows, and throughout the programme itself when more and more successes are achieved and benefits realised, this team should be increased to involve a wider range of people and functions. Conscious attention should be given to managing a formal and informal network that forms the basis of a guiding coalition, asking the questions 'Do we have the right people on board?' and, if not, 'Who should we have on board?'

Example

In one Service Management implementation, a project steering committee was created comprised solely of line managers. Buy-in and commitment from the operational level was lacking. This team was not seen as credible and did not demand respect. Progress was slow and there was much negative energy and resistance to the programme.

Well-respected operational team leaders and experienced people were then taken from various departments to form a nucleus of Change Agents. These people were sent on Service Management training, leadership training and were given the freedom to hire an external consultant and pick team members to drive the Change through. This group had peer respect and was motivated to making the Service Management improvements happen within their departments.

5.3.3 Creating a vision

The guiding coalition should be responsible for ensuring that a vision is produced describing the aim and purpose of the CSIP. A good vision statement can serve four important purposes: clarify the direction of the programme, motivate people to take action in the right direction, coordinate the actions of many different people and outline the aims of senior management (see also Chapter 2). Without a sensible and easily understood vision, a Service Management implementation programme can easily dissolve into a list of confusing, incompatible projects that can take the organisation in the wrong direction, or even nowhere at all. A vision that is easy to understand is also easy to explain. As a rule of thumb, if one cannot explain the vision in five minutes, the vision itself is not clear and focused enough.

A sound vision statement is important when forming a business justification for a CSIP – if one is already underway then having clear aims will help set more specific goals. The goals of the CSIP should be 'SMART' (Specific, Measurable, Achievable, Realistic and Time-related) as well as being addressed in terms relating to the business itself.

5.3.4   Communicating the vision

As stated in Section 2.2, although the vision is a powerful tool in helping guide and coordinate Change, the real power is unleashed when the vision is effectively communicated to the stakeholders. Section 2.2 also points out that the vision should be understandable by every stakeholder. The way it is communicated should be aimed at specific target groups. For example, communication to senior management will require a different approach to communication to IT staff.

Another important aspect of the communication is 'walking the talk' – demonstrating by example. It is a fact of life that people tend to copy what management *does* rather than what it *says*.

Example

The IT director addressed all IT employees in the canteen on the start of a Service Management program. He said: 'In two years' time we will have fully implemented IT Service Management'. Nobody had a clue what his statement meant. Had he addressed it in a more practical way, specifying it in terms of understandable and achievable quick wins, he would have gained more interest and motivation.

5.3.5   Empowering others to act on the vision

As stated in Section 2.3, establishing the urgency, creating a guiding coalition, creating and communicating a vision are all aimed at creating energy, enthusiasm, buy-in and commitment to make Change happen. In the empowering phase two important aspects need to be stressed, i.e. 'enabling' and 'removing barriers'. There needs to be new, changed or added facilities so that people are really able to make the Change happen.

Hint

There is no point telling the Service Desk to shorten the resolution times of incidents while the Service Desk people complain about the quality of the Service Management tool being used.

The people responsible for making the CSIP a success should ask themselves the question 'What do I need to do to enable all involved to make this Change a success?' Another simple check is 'Do you now feel able to carry through the Change?'

5.3.6 Planning for and creating quick wins

Implementing Service Management improvements can be a lengthy Programme of Change. It is important that, during the programme, quick wins are communicated and realised. Short-term wins help to keep a change effort on track and help keep the energy and commitment levels high. Real transformation takes time. Without quick wins, too many people give up or join the ranks of those opposing the Change.

Quick wins can also be used to help:

- convince Change sceptics of the benefits
- retain support of influential stakeholders
- expand the guiding coalition and get more people on board and committed to the programme
- build confidence to tackle even more complex implementation issues and process integration.

Try to identify some quick wins for each process and plan these into the CSIP. It is also important that quick wins are made visible and are communicated to all stakeholders. When planning to communicate the quick wins, obtain answers to the questions 'For whom is it a quick win?' and 'To what degree does it support the overall aims and goals?' and work these answers into the communication.

Example

Issue
Customers were complaining that they never received advance information about what was happening. The systems were taken down for the implementation of a Change without prior notice to Users.

Quick win
A Forward Schedule of Change was produced and made available to User group representatives.

Issue
A particular application was causing numerous problems and additional work for the support specialists, and causing irritation to the Users.

Quick win
A pilot problem analysis team was put in place to identify and remove known errors causing outages.

Issue
Lack of any management information relating to support calls.

Quick win
Manual Incident registration, classification and reporting was established and an incident team meeting introduced at the start of each shift. The team quickly identified some recurring incidents, work-arounds and a suggestion for a priority mechanism for handling incidents. They quickly became more effective and able to develop new suggestions for improvements.

5.3.7 Consolidating improvements and producing more Change

The success of quick wins keeps the momentum going and creates more Change. In a CSIP it is important to recognise short, middle and longer term wins. Changes should sink deeply into the new culture or the new approaches will be fragile and subject to regression:

- quick wins have the characteristics of 'convincing',' motivating' and showing immediate benefits and gains

- medium-term wins have the characteristics of 'confidence' and 'capability' – and having a set of working processes in place

- longer-term goals have the characteristics of 'self-learning' and 'expertise' and fully integrated processes that have self-learning and improvement built into them; reaching this stage requires a baseline of confident, capable delivery and real understanding – trying to reach this level before having gone through the other levels is like trying to win an Olympic medal before training has commenced.

5.3.8 Institutionalising the Change

Change needs to be institutionalised within the organisation. Many Changes fail because they are not consolidated into everyday practice. To institutionalise a Change means showing how new working practices have produced real gain and benefits, and ensuring that the improvements are embedded in all organisational practices.

Often the CSIP project team is disbanded before the working practices are institutionalised; there is a danger that people may revert to old working practices.

Some ways of institutionalising Changes:

- new recruitment and selection criteria (looking to hire people with ITIL experience or proven Customer or service focused experience)

- new employee (business and IT) induction includes IT Service Management familiarisation: 'This is the way we do things.'

- employee training plans and offerings include ITIL or Service Management focused training

- process goals and management reporting is matched to changing requirements, showing that they are used and requests are made for new sets of steering information

- clear actions defined in minutes of meetings based upon reports produced

- new IT solutions and development projects are integrated into existing processes.

Signs that the Changes have been institutionalised include:

- people defend the procedures and declare, 'This is the way we work', rather than, 'This is the way I've been told to do it'

- people make suggestions for improving procedures and work instructions to make them more effective or efficient

- process owners are proud of their achievements and offer to give presentations and write articles

- people come back from ITIL conferences and seminars and declare, 'I didn't learn much that we haven't already done or thought of'.

5.4 Managing cultural Changes

5.4.1 Culture

According to the Framework for Change and the eight steps to manage Organisational Change, implementing Service Management also affects the culture of the organisation. In fact culture is at the heart of the matter – a key issue – in implementing Service Management. Culture could support an implementation or it could be the source of resistance. This being the case, it is surprising that many organisations do not view managing cultural Change as one of their top priorities. Too often when an organisation starts a CSIP, the new organisational structure and technology gets the bulk of the attention and almost no attention is given to the effect of the implementation on the organisational culture. Organisational culture affects leadership or leadership style and, as stated in Section 5.3, leadership affects the chances of success of an Organisational Change.

For the implementation project to succeed and to get the results defined before starting implementation it is very important to give attention to organisational culture, especially when there is more than one part of the organisation involved. Although culture is an intangible aspect, it has to be managed. The main issues to consider are how to:

■ determine culture

■ define supportive behaviour

■ change undesirable culture

■ deal with resistance.

5.4.2 Changing culture

Organisational culture is comprised of the ideas, corporate values, beliefs, practices, expectations about behaviour and attitudes that are shared by the employees and management in an organisation. Deep-seated beliefs are mostly taken for granted by long-term employees, so it might be wise to ask newer employees about their experiences in working in this organisation. Additional information can frequently be gleaned from anyone who is not too closely involved in the organisation. This will certainly include suppliers and Customers, who can more easily be questioned by an appropriately worded satisfaction survey.

Proposed Organisational Changes affect people and the way they feel. Sometimes the proposed Change leads to a split between two parties: those who initiate the Change and those who are the object of the Change. A case of perpetrators and victims, it looks like war – a war which has to be won to realise the good cause. The parties may differ in their perspective of the cause. An organisation may be strongly divided. This division produces symptoms such as vagueness, public resistance, scepticism, cynicism and sabotage, and could lead to valuable staff leaving the organisation. Where these symptoms are displayed, knowledge, experience and energy remain unused or may be lost forever. However in times of radical Changes these emotions could just as easily be channelled to benefit a Change. Feelings have an important impact on the outcome of an Organisational Change.

5.4.3   Manage feelings

From an IT management perspective, managing Changes has little to do with feelings. IT management has more to do with the gap between software development and IT management, resourcing problems, lifecycle management of systems, integration of activities, Customer focus, a shorter time to market and so on. Many Organisational Changes are started precisely to resolve these problems. Familiar habits, methods, and procedures are altered and it is at this time that staff may feel concerned about the Change. What are the concerns and how can they be managed?

According to Elizabeth Kübler-Ross people react according to a specific pattern. There are two dimensions involved: time and moods. Over time, one sees changes in mood, and the available energy diminishes and increases. One can recognise six stages as depicted in Figure 5.3.

1 Denial

2 Anger

3 Negotiation to restore the *old* situation

4 Dip/acceptance of the inevitable

5 Exploring the possibilities of the new situation

6 Integration in daily habits.

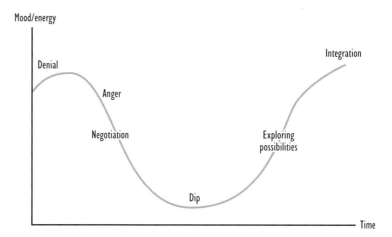

Figure 5.3 – The utilisation curve of Kübler-Ross

This curve will differ from person to person in time and intensity.

> **Example**
>
> Bad experiences with management can create a lot of resistance (anger) and therefore one might want to focus some resources into better training for management or reassigning those that prove to be barriers.

5.4.4   Transformation cascade

Changes with great impact are usually initiated from the top. Starting from the strategic level in an organisation the 'Change' is handed down to the tactical level and then to an operational level. It is more the rule than the exception that each level goes through its own 'transformation process'. The outcome of this process is the cause and often the demand for the next level in an organisation to transform. Information about this process and how people are dealing with it are seldom handed down. Unfortunately the higher level gives little feedback about this process to the next level. One could visualise it as a 'transformation cascade' as shown in Figure 5.4.

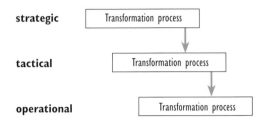

Figure 5.4 – Transformation cascade

What also happens is that the content of the vision and reasons for the Organisational Change becomes more and more vague as it moves down through the organisation. Only parts of the rationale behind the Organisational Change comes through to the operational level. Figure 5.5 depicts the fact that only part of the original content of the vision is handed down ('the shadow of the upper level') to the operational level. The clarity and content of the communication is further blurred as the message is passed through the organisational levels.

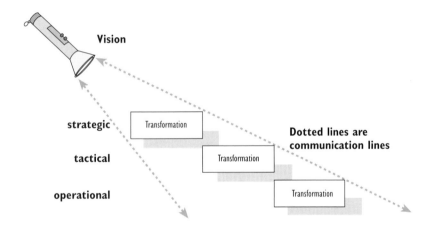

Figure 5.5 – Communication becomes blurred

The outcome of each level having its own separate transformation processes is that each fails to appreciate the feelings of the other. This is most evident for staff at the operational level, who feel particularly 'put-upon' if they have not been involved in the discussions. And yet it is the commitment and energy of the operational level that are essential to the success of any Organisational Change.

5.4.5   Relevance to Service Management implementation

Any implementation of Service Management will require the organisation to embark on a programme of Organisational Change, but, sometimes, the Change Programme fails to realise the desired results. One reason for this is the underestimation of the scale of work required. Support staff, Users and Customers will have to adopt new working practices. When any new tool or process is introduced, there may be initial enthusiasm for the new approach. The results, however, may be that, in time, unfamiliar working practices, teething troubles and no significant quick wins may have a negative effect on the balance between costs and benefits[2]. A drop in benefits will soon be matched with a drop in enthusiasm of the staff involved. The support staff involved may lose interest and the rationale behind the Change may then be challenged. In time, according to the pattern of Kübler-Ross, workers become angry and sabotage the Service Management implementation project with the aim of stopping the project and getting back to the old regime. With such attitudes prevailing, expect to see project members who fail to attend meetings, failure to deliver results at specified deadlines and so on. One could even see, as Eli Goldratt portrayed in his Theory Of Constraints[3], symptoms like his six elements of resistance to change:

1 Disagreement with the reasons for Service Management implementation

2 Disagreement with the direction of the Service Management solution

3 Lack of faith in the completeness or maturity of the solution

4 Fear of negative consequences generated from the solution ('Now my colleagues can see what the results are of my daily work', as one appointed process manager once said)

5 Too many obstacles on the road to reach a solution

6 Not knowing what to do.

It is imperative that quick wins are planned into any Service Management implementation project to build enthusiasm so that staff can explore the new possibilities of the new situation. Improvements should become consolidated and institutionalised into the new approach.

5.4.6   Managing communication

Example

Every manager knows that communication is essential, certainly when an Organisational Change, such as a Service Management implementation, is involved. So a conference is held, the new organisational structure is presented, the new blueprint is handed down, everybody gets a newsletter and life goes on. Management believes the communication issue has been resolved. And yet, after some time rumours start circulating and people become annoyed by the lack of information.

[2] This text is an extension to the implementation considerations of the OGC *Service Support* book, Paragraph 4.3.9 – the 'silver bullet' lifecycle.

[3] The Theory of Constraints (TOC) is an overall philosophy developed by Dr. Eliyahu M. Goldratt, portrayed in his bestseller book *The Goal*, usually applied to running and improving an organisation. The theory in essence is based on finding the real bottlenecks (constraints) by simply asking the questions 'What is the constraint?' and 'Is it the real cause or just a symptom of something else?' Through asking these questions systematically and recurrently, one comes to the real cause. Don't forget that in life generally, as in Service Management, the main thing that limits our freedom of choice is the unspoken thoughts or assumptions that we have. So by asking this question over and over again we become aware of the real cause why a Service Management implementation hasn't succeeded (yet). The more open we are to check the validity of our assumptions, the more freedom we have and the more secure we feel.

What every manager must appreciate is that communication is not a one-time issue but an ongoing requirement to ensure that the initial enthusiasm is maintained and enhanced. A lot of organisations make the classic mistake of stopping communication in an attempt to avoid putting out messages that are ambiguous or might provide material for rumours. The effect of such a decision may be opposite of what one was aiming at: people lose interest or resistance to Change may rise. Communication tends to reduce uncertainty and stress, even when the Organisational Change means bad news for them. Not knowing where one stands is worse than getting bad news.

It is important to get everyone involved in thinking about why an Organisational Change is needed; let them give their views on how to get to 'Where we want to be' (how the Change could succeed) and the consequences are of the Change ('What's in it for me?'). If everyone is involved, communication between the levels and feedback on views will be accomplished. Because the feelings become apparent, there is room for discussion about doubts and objections. By having this direct feedback it is easier to come to terms with the issues and this can accelerate and make the Organisational Change more effective in the long run.

5.4.7   Resistance to Change

People differ greatly in their adaptability to Change. Resistance is often seen as a barrier to Change. One key mistake is to ignore resistance and force it 'underground'. But in these times, when IT specialists are a much sought after group of professionals, treating them with such a lack of respect may be enough to make them look for another job.

It is also important to distinguish between negative and positive criticism and resistance.

> **Example**
>
> Negative resistance includes statement like:
>
> - 'This is a waste of time – it'll never work.'
>
> - 'I don't believe a word of it.'
>
> - 'I've seen it all before and I don't want anything to do with it.'
>
> These will need to be changed by demonstrating benefits.
>
> Alternatively:
>
> - 'That'll never work because…'
>
> - 'I want to believe you but…'
>
> are both positive criticisms – 'because…' may mean that the individual has positive advice and another way of suggesting an improved way of working while 'I want to believe you but….' can indicate commitment if certain barriers or obstacles are removed.

Making resistance open and discussing and analysing it can help identify additional areas of empowerment or additional barriers that need removing. Remember, however, that, if a framework is created for capturing and discussing resistance, the organisation must be committed to doing something with the feedback. If there is no action taken as a result then any positive resistance can quickly turn to additional negative resistance. This is a prime case of management needing to 'walk the talk' to gain trust and commitment.

Example

In one organisation, trust was low and commitment was lacking: 'We've heard it all before'. An investigation was carried out to identify what employees saw as key barriers and problem areas and to obtain suggestions for operational improvements that they felt were necessary. A list of issues was raised, prioritised and, whenever possible, immediately addressed or carried through to the CSIP to address.

Issues

– 'Anybody can walk into the support area with a request.'

– 'Customers phone numerous times to different people.'

– 'We have to go into the computer room every time we want to check status.'

Management immediately initiated a restricted access area and a formalised method of making requests:

– A centralised call system was promised as part of the CSIP.

– Monitors were immediately provided in the support room.

The immediate actions and investment from management had the effect of convincing the employees that they were being taken seriously and some quick wins were made.

Typically, almost half of the people involved are neutral to Organisational Changes. At one extreme there will be the 'early adopters' who could be the ambassadors for the Change and at the other extreme there will be the doubters – people who are resistant to Change. It may well be less effective to address all the energy to the doubters. As a rule of thumb 20% of the total population will absorb 80% of the energy but are resistant to Change. Focus, therefore, on the 80% of the population who are positive or neutral to the Change. But it is also important to ensure that this group represents all sectors of the organisation, so that it has the integrity to attract doubters in the fullness of time, rather than merely pick the staff that happen to be available at the time.

5.5 Roles for implementation

One of the most difficult aspects in implementing a CSIP is the fact that the new processes and working practices are implemented within an existing organisational structure. The implementation of Service Management practices introduces new roles into the organisation that may overlap traditional organisational boundaries.

5.5.1   Authority matrix

A characteristic of a process is that all related activities need not necessarily be limited to one specific organisational unit. Configuration Management activities, for example, can be conducted in departments such as computer operations, system programming, Application Management, Network Management, systems development and even non-IT departments like procurement, storehouse or accounting. Since processes and their activities run through a whole organisation, the activities should be mapped to the existing IT departments or sections and coordinated by process managers. Once detailed procedures and work instructions have been developed, an organisation has to map its staff to the activities of the process. Clear definitions of accountability and responsibility are critical success factors for any CSIP. Without this, roles and responsibilities within the new process can be confusing, and individuals might revert to how the activities were handled before the new procedures were put in place.

To assist with this task the A.R.C.I model is often used within organisations indicating roles and responsibilities in relation to processes and activities:

- A – accountability – ownership of quality, and end result of process
- R – responsibility – correct execution of process and activities
- C – consulted – involvement through input of knowledge and information
- I – informed – receiving information about process execution and quality.

Example

An organisation planned to implement Change Management. It was decided to start with a workshop with the key stakeholders within the IT department: the various IT managers. They drew up a map of all the Change Management activities and mapped them to the IT sections. They came to an agreement on which section was accountable, who should be responsible, who should be consulted and who should be informed. After that a blueprint was set up to clarify the goal, scope, activities (with allocation of roles) and the necessary input and output were defined. This blueprint was authorised by the stakeholders and communicated across the whole organisation.

It is important to understand the distinction between a formal function within an organisation and the process roles that the function is expected to carry out. A formal function may fulfil more than one specific Service Management role and carry out activities relating to more than one process. In the following example, a formal function 'Network administrator' is 'Responsible' for carrying out 'Incident Management' as well as 'Capacity Management' activities. Although the Network administrator may report to a functional line manager he or she is also responsible for carrying out activities for the Service Desk and Capacity Management process owners.

This is a difficult and time-consuming exercise but one that helps clarify, to all involved, which activities they are expected to fulfil, as well as identifying any gaps in process delivery and responsibilities. An example of how this should be done is provided in Table 5.1.

Function:	Client	Service Desk Manager	Network Administrator/ System manager	Service Desk Analysts	Senior IT Management	Supplier
Incident Management						
Incident Alerted Notification	R/I	A	I	I	I	I
Information Recorded	I	A	R	R		
Incident Classification		A/I	R/C	R/C	C	
Incident Diagnoses		A/C	R	R		C
Initial support Initial Investigation Resolution Recovery Escalation	C	A/I	C	C		
Further Support Detailed Investigation Resolution Recovery	C/I	A/C/I	R	R	C	R/C
Incident follow-up	C	A/R	C	R	C	
Incident Closure	I	A/I	I	R		
Monitoring	I	A/I	I	R	I	
Proactive communication	C/I	A/R		R		
Process Review	C/I	A/R	C	C	R	C
Capacity Management						
Monitoring performance Monitoring log files and system counters		I	R	I		

Table 5.1 – Example A.R.C.I. model authority matrix

As can be seen, there is only one person accountable for an activity, although several people may be responsible for carrying out parts of the activity. In this example, the Service Desk Management is fully accountable for the whole Incident Management process, although informed and helped by other functions. Accountable means to have the end-responsibility for the process. So, in this example, the Service Desk Management must understand where the process is now and where it is going, with specific detailed key performance indicators set up to monitor the health and progress of this process. Note here that, in Capacity Management, no Authority has been identified.

Possible problems to watch for with the A.R.C.I model:

■ more than one person accountable for a process which means in practice no-one is accountable

■ delegation of responsibility without necessary authority

■ focus on matching processes and activities with departments

■ wrong division/combination of functions

■ combination of accountability for closely related processes, such as Incident Management, Problem Management, Configuration Management, Change Management and Release Management.

5.5.2   ITIL and the existing organisational structure

Can a process model be applied to the existing organisational structure? In many real life Service Management implementation cases there is a friction between the existing organisational structure and the new process approach. Should one adopt a new organisational matrix structure with line and process responsibilities separated? Who is in the end accountable? Should one separate the operational and tactical processes and map them to different IT units?

To organise Service Management dealing with ten processes in a well-balanced organisational structure is complex. Many units play a part in the activities (see the example in Table 5.1). It is necessary to have a single line of command (accountability) to integrate these activities across organisational boundaries. Process managers tend to be functionally, and not hierarchically, responsible for the IT employees of different units. Practice has shown that several problems may arise:

- IT employees aren't used to having two lines of command, the line and process manager (two captains on a ship)

- line managers themselves are not used to having 'someone looking over their shoulder'

- process managers do not have enough formal status and authority to earn the respect of the IT employees, and so the employees in return neglect the work to be done for the process

- danger of increased overheads can be created if process managers are also participating in the management team (which they should)

- communication between the line and process manager may be insufficient or even break down.

Besides a matrix organisational structure, there are many other organisational structures that can be made to work for IT Service Management. These include the integration of line and process responsibilities in one manager and the separation of:

- standard and non-standard IT service provision

- current and new IT service provision (projects)

- operational and tactical processes

- front office (Customer relationship) and back office (execution)

- different IT infrastructure platforms

- different IT specialities.

Which guiding organisational principle is applied may differ from organisation to organisation. Each principle has its own benefits and drawbacks. There is no universal organisational structure for IT Service Management. In a CSIP several other criteria could also be taken into account and applied to a new organisational structure, including guidelines for:

- maximum numbers of staff in a unit or team

- span of control for line and process managers

- communication lines and direct supervision between units

- authority for *all* individuals' interests

- educational level and ambition of the employees – be aware that some people like having a clear-cut line of command, others do not

- line managers to coordinate with process managers.

Also consider:

- ranking of line managers and process owners (they should be equal)
- whether the current culture is helpful to a new process-oriented way of working
- whether there are plans for the outsourcing some IT activities to an internal or external third party
- governance, reporting and meeting lines – if there are going to be separate meetings for process management then what is its authority in comparison with line management?
- costs of recruiting and selecting new (process) managers and employees, costs of employees leaving the organisation, less productivity and turmoil at the start of a new organisational structure.

Several other principles, i.e. political feasibility, may also apply when setting up an organisational structure to implement Service Management processes. The principles mentioned are not unique to the implementation of Service Management processes. However they are relevant for a successful transformation.

5.6 Training

> **Quote**
>
> **'I keep six honest serving men, they taught me all I know.**
>
> **Their names are Who, Why, What, When, How and Where.'**
>
> **Rudyard Kipling**

For anyone considering undertaking, commissioning or delivering training of any description there can be no better guidance than the above from Rudyard Kipling. Obviously the approach to the task(s) may differ from organisation to organisation and from individual to individual. However the concept of transferring or exchanging knowledge (information) in order to achieve understanding and then elicit a response remains the same.

5.6.1 Benefits of training

Structured training initiatives in a CSIP will provide the following benefits in addition to skills and competence development:

- speed up the time to realise the intended benefits of the CSIP and maximise the chance of overall programme success
- create overall awareness and understanding of the framework and terminology
- provide a platform where the relevance of the new learning for the organisation can be discussed in groups
- provide a platform and knowledge to help identify and minimise possible problems and incorrect implementation approaches

- help highlight skills and competence deficiencies so that additional skills and competence development initiatives can be taken (such as coaching, soft skills development)
- provide a pool of process-trained resources.

5.6.2   Why train?

Section 3.2 describes the Framework for Change, clearly showing people, their skills and their abilities as a crucial element for any CSIP. As such, adequate attention needs to be placed on enabling the people through effective skills and competence development:

- Why do people need training?
- What will the organisation get out of it?
- How much will it cost?

The biggest investment most organisations will make will be in the people they employ to deliver the products or services of that organisation to the Customer. It is not unnatural therefore for organisations to want to see a return on the investment in training.

The service tenet of 'Do it right the first time and then better the second time with only minimal or justifiable increase in cost' can be applied in this 'Why train?' scenario. In a service environment delivery starts with the first contact, and goes right through to the Customer satisfaction figures. Every member of the organisation is involved in the delivery of the product or service. Everyone has ownership for getting it right. An organisation that seems unwilling to invest in structural training programmes in support of CSIPs must ask themselves, 'What if we don't train?', 'What will be the consequences?', and 'What will be the likelihood of success with our CSIP?'

Viewed from the trainee perspective, training could be seen as a reward for their efforts during the previous period or as a welcome relief from the pressures of the working day. Training is not a reward or relief – it is a 'must-have' in order to deliver a quality product or service. Understanding, not only of the organisation's needs, but also the Customer's needs, can lead to a more productive and responsive workforce.

From the organisation's perspective training is sometimes seen in a far more monetary sense. In some cases it is expensive and the return is unclear. However, a better-trained and informed workforce will be more flexible, responsive and ultimately more productive because they understand both the business and Customer's needs.

This can be even more important when establishing a new service, product or business. The principles of Service Management are equally applicable in an IT environment as in a private home. In the home, when the heating system breaks down, the engineering centre is called and they take the details and allocate an engineer to call at a certain time. In the office, when a PC breaks, the first call is to the Service Desk, who takes the details and then manages a resolution within an agreed timescale. The difference is only in the terminology.

Where is the Customer in all this? What do they want from a service provider? Elements like flexibility, responsiveness, understanding, empathy, and product knowledge are the common things. It is therefore incumbent on the service provider organisation to ensure their workforce has the appropriate skills, knowledge and understanding to deliver what the Customer expects. Obviously this means keeping up-to-date with business, Customer and industry trends and best practices. The ultimate objective is an increase in Customer satisfaction – the more the Customer is satisfied the more they will wish to use the services.

5.6.3   Who to train

Determining who to train starts with the job role and responsibilities of each individual. A training needs analysis can be performed to match the requirements of the role and organisation against the skills of the individual. Once the areas of weakness are identified, a matrix of who requires training in what areas can be devised.

A further consideration on who to train must be concerned with the business needs of the organisation and the Customer. It is of little use training people to understand technical issues if they cannot relate that knowledge to a process that in turn is related to providing a service to a Customer.

> **Example**
>
> The first point of contact with the Customer is typically the Service Desk. What skills and knowledge are needed here? 'Soft' skills are certainly required, such as answering the telephone, good communication skills and so on. Harder skills, such as technical knowledge, process knowledge, and business understanding, are also needed. All elements are required to make a successful Service Desk analyst. The technical side is easily identified and sourced from manufacturers, vendors and third parties.

Now, what of the processes involved? Service Management provides a generic set of 'best practice' process and activity descriptions necessary to deliver effective Service Desk service provision. There is a very clear view of what is expected of a Service Desk in terms of recording, analysing, assigning and subsequent tracking of a service or component failure with the objective of restoring normal service as quickly as possible. As can be seen in the ARCI model in Table 5.1, a number of people are involved in these activity sets from different parts of the organisation. As such any training programme must be sure to involve all those who play a role in carrying out the activity sets.

One of the more technical aspects of service provision could be seen as that of Problem Management. The concept here is twofold:

1   Reactively – root cause analysis to identify what has broken in order that it can subsequently be fixed

2   Proactively – either to prevent failure from occurring or accepting failure will occur to prevent them from recurring.

Here ITIL again gives some guidance on the type of process to be followed and its relationships with other processes.

Each area of the service provider organisation will need to have process and procedure in place to govern the way it operates on a day-to-day basis. Subsequently each of these areas will require the correct level of knowledge and skill in process and procedure. There can be no better way to achieve this understanding than to use industry best practice as a guide and starting point. Each area (or discipline) will then be able to develop its own specific processes and procedures in line with organisation needs and Customer expectations. For the Service Desk example above it is also important to note that those involved in the various Service Desk activities may require different levels of Service Desk training. Accredited ITIL training organisations offer a range of training possibilities for both Service Desk operations and for Service Desk Management. These will include a brief overview from Foundation level to specific process and to full manager's training in IT Service Management.

As a general rule, those with more responsibility, authority or accountability for a process will require more in-depth training. For example, the Service Desk Manager may undergo full manager's training in IT Service Management to understand and ensure the integration with other key processes such as Change Management, Problem Management and Configuration Management. The Service Desk Manager also undergoes ITIL Service Desk practitioner training to gain the skills required for shaping and managing the Service Desk processes.

5.6.4   When to train

There are many alternatives for when to train: at the beginning of an individual's employment, as and when required, only when something new is introduced, when a process or procedure is introduced or amended, or in an ongoing way that meets the business needs and the Customer's expectations.

Each of these is, of course, valid in some situations. It is certainly important to train new staff in organisational procedures when they first join the organisation – that is the purpose of Induction Training. But this is only the first stage of what can be seen as a combination of specific and ongoing activities. Typically this is easiest in a technical environment when progression through the various levels of technical competency can be more easily measured. However in a service provision environment the measurement of progression and competence is perhaps not so easy to measure. The establishment and maintenance of a Training Programme is therefore fundamental in the provision of skills and knowledge.

In a CSIP, 'awareness training' is one of the key success factors in empowering employees to develop processes and procedures. This will also establish a common framework and shared terminology for a broad audience (of stakeholders) and more in-depth knowledge for those charged with developing new working practices.

The major stages in developing a programme can be seen as:

- specify roles, including the skill and knowledge requirements for the role
- establish the number of training stages by examination of the role specification to identify the scope of the training required in the programme, and the most appropriate order of training
- specify the training requirements, of the individuals as well as the programme, to be covered in each stage of the programme
- determine relevant experience of the individual against the role specification as this may modify the training requirements of each stage (e.g. an existing employee moving roles will not require Induction Training)
- identify the training resources including facilities (internal or external) that are available, to be involved in on-the-job training and the contribution this will make to the whole programme
- identify the target duration of the programme, influenced by the organisation's need, individual experience and Customer expectations.

The objective of any training programme is to ensure that the individual achieves the required levels of competence in all aspects of their role in the shortest possible time and at an acceptable cost to the employer.

Competence can be checked by systematic appraisal of the individual's progress, not only by their supervisor, but also by themselves. This progress checking can be aided by comparison with a pre-defined set of criteria such as the ITIL examinations that are recognised worldwide. It is therefore possible to ensure that ITIL training is built into any training programme knowing that formal examinations will ensure that satisfactory progress is being made.

Cost can be checked by ensuring that the training programme is still relevant to the individual's role. A regular review of the whole programme to cater for Changes in processes, practices, procedure, business needs and Customer expectations must be carried out. The training programme can then be adapted to meet these Changes.

A typical programme may cover anything up to two years initially depending on the skills and experience of the individual. A sample programme is depicted in Figure 5.6 that assumes no previous skills and knowledge of an IT service organisation.

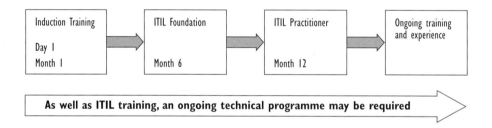

Figure 5.6 – Sample training programme

It follows that training, especially in an IT service organisation, cannot be a one-off activity. It must be an ongoing activity (or group of activities) tied to the individual's requirements, skills, and knowledge aligned to the organisation needs and the Customer expectations.

5.6.5   How to train

Consideration needs to be given to training methods (classroom, on the job) as well as the training levels (e.g. Basic and Advanced). There are five main training methods:

1   External training courses

2   In-house training courses

3   Programmed learning (Computer Based Training (CBT), distance learning, e-training)

4   Tutorial or seminar sessions (especially for a particular topic)

5   On-the-job training.

Which of these to use will depend on a number of factors ranging from the individual and their needs to the business and Customer needs of the organisation. Training is not just a single activity at one time. Rather it is a combination of a number of activities coming together in an ongoing manner to achieve a series of objectives.

5.6.6   External training courses

Vendors, independent training bodies or even local colleges can conduct these courses, but:

- for ITIL training, only organisations that have been accredited by an ITIL examining body are recommended
- for an individual to deliver ITIL training they should similarly be accredited and accepted by the examining body that accredits the training organisation.

There is no restriction on where the ITIL training can take place so it can be either on-site at the organisation's own training facility or off-site at a facility provided by the training organisation. Another advantage of these training courses is the certification test at the end. The students MUST learn something, in order to complete the certification, which can be mandatory to subsequent work or promotion!

5.6.7   In-house training courses

For Induction and ongoing organisation-specific training the use of in-house facilities and training departments, should they exist, is sensible and cost-effective. But ITIL training could also be part of an in-house programme. The advantage here is that Service Management concepts can be structured to suit an organisation's specific need. However this does mean that no formal examination would be available. The use of properly accredited staff from within an organisation would allow for in-house training courses to be more cost-effective, assuming that the organisation was also accredited as a training provider. Training in ITIL can of course be carried as part of an in-house programme and then an external examination could be arranged. Consideration should be given to the benefits of external training against in-house training. External training will give the opportunity to exchange experience and ideas with people from other organisations but is likely to be more costly.

External training providers can be used to help facilitate an in-house training programme. There are some advantages to this approach, as the tutor can bring some personal experience to the course that would provide some added value.

5.6.8   Programmed learning (CBT, distance learning, e-training)

If the organisation has the facilities then this type of training can be an acceptable approach. However, there are disadvantages to this approach including the loss of peer-to-peer exchanges.

5.6.9   Tutorial or seminar sessions (especially for a particular topic)

As ITIL is made up of processes covering all areas of IT Service Management it is perfectly acceptable to use these topics as the subject of seminar and tutorial sessions. An organisation using this method can gain the advantage of understanding ITIL and then working with the presenter to understand how the process can be adapted to meet specific needs. It is, of course, possible that the presenter can, with some prior knowledge of the service organisation, develop the session from the outset to be specific to the organisation. This is especially useful when introducing ITIL into an organisation for the first time.

5.6.10 On-the-job training

The very direct focus that planned on-the-job training can bring to the programme cannot be over-emphasised. However on its own it is doubtful if the full value of training can be achieved. This type of training is arguably best when it is complemented by a formal classroom activity. In order to achieve ITIL training in this way the person doing the training must have been trained to the appropriate level in ITIL and must have the necessary experience in the discipline or role.

5.6.11 What to train

Training will include:

- ITIL
- people ('soft') skills: communication, listening, negotiation skills
- ITSM supporting tools
- procedures and working instructions.

5.7 Use of tools

It is generally recognised that the use of Service Management tools is essential for the success of all but the very smallest process implementations. However, it is important that the tool being used must support the processes – not the other way around. After considering the level of maturity of the processes ('Where are we now?') and the ambitions the organisation has ('Where do we want to be?'), it may deduced that the Service Management tool(s) already in place may no longer be adequate. As was stated in Section 4.5, it then becomes necessary to generate a new Statement of Requirements (SOR) and a new selection process will commence. Appendix L provides more details on the selection and use of tools.

6 HOW DO WE CHECK OUR MILESTONES HAVE BEEN REACHED?

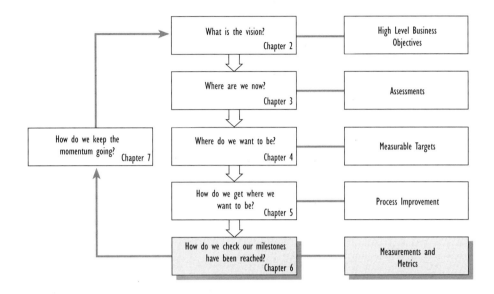

To judge process performance, clearly defined objectives with measurable targets should be set. Confirmation needs to be sought that these objectives and the milestones set in the Continuous Service Improvement Programme (CSIP) have been reached and that the desired improvement in service quality has been achieved. At the completion of each significant stage of the programme a Post Implementation Review (PIR) should be conducted to ensure the objectives have been met. The PIR will include a review of supporting documentation and the general awareness amongst staff of the refined processes. A comparison is required of what has been achieved against the original goals set in the project. Once this has been confirmed new improvement targets should be defined. As previously mentioned, the basic process for a CSIP is to assess the current situation, design improvement and implement the new process. Before rolling out to the live community it is essential the new process is first tested and then a controlled Pilot is undertaken to ensure the desired effect is being achieved.

To confirm that the milestones have been reached Key Performance Indicators (KPIs) will need to be constantly monitored. These KPIs will include Customer satisfaction targets so there will be a need to survey Customers at various stages throughout the CSIP to confirm that Changes made are improving the Customer perception of the service quality. It is possible that the services have higher availability, that there are fewer incidents and that response times have improved but at the same time the Customer's perception of service quality has not improved. Clearly this is as important and will need to be addressed by talking to Customers to ascertain their concerns. Confirmation will need to be sought that CSIPs put in place are addressing the Customer's primary needs.

Example

In a recent study of IT directors in the Netherlands, 70% had strategic IT plans aligned to business strategic direction, yet less than 50% said they actually measured results of strategic planning roll-out.

Customer Satisfaction Surveys (CSS) can be conducted either by regular formal surveys or by use of areas such as the Service Desk where randomly selected callers can be asked a small number of questions on their perception of the quality of the service. If the Service Desk surveys are performed then the information gathered should be considered as supplementary to that gathered by the full CSS. Very careful consideration must be made as to the wording of questions and to the actual questions asked. Questions should concentrate on the areas that are important to the Customer and should start with the most important such as a question about value for money or service reliability. It is also important that when people give their time to take part in these type of surveys they are given the results of them. This feedback should also contain details of proposed action to address any poor scores or comments made.

> **Hint**
>
> **It may be difficult to get enough Customers to take part in a CSS and a variety of methods have been tried to encourage people such as gifts or donations to charity. A better way is to agree this at the time that the SLAs are negotiated and to actual document this as a target in the SLA. For example:**
>
> **'The IT Service provider will conduct full and formal CSS every 6 months and results will be fed back to the Customer within 1 month to include CSIP actions. The Customer undertakes to ensure that 90% of CSS forms (on the Intranet) are completed within 2 weeks of them being received.'**

The results of the CSS will need to be trended with a target of continual improvement in Customer Perception Ratings.

Throughout the CSIP, assessment should identify whether the targets have been achieved and, if so, whether new targets, and therefore new KPIs, need to be defined. If they have been achieved but the perception has not improved, then new targets may need to be set and measures put in place to ensure that these are being met. Detailed in Section 6.1 are examples of KPIs that could be monitored for all the processes. Every organisation will have to decide which of these KPIs are applicable to them and if there are others that they need to collect. Different KPIs may be required for each of the stakeholders detailed in Section 2.2 and Paragraph 3.5.1. For example, performance indicators will differ at an organisational level to a team level and to an individual.

Several of the indicators will be difficult to monitor and collect without the use of the appropriate tool. So an important factor when selecting tools is to consider their ability to analyse the KPI data and to easily produce the required management information. It will be very difficult and time consuming to produce trended reports to show the efficiency of the Incident Management process, for example, by manual analysis. The appropriate toolset, possibly interfaced with a report-writing tool, should greatly reduce the time required to produce reports and ensure a high level of accuracy.

Process owners will require very regular reports, probably monthly, based on their CSFs and KPIs and others within the organisation will also require these reports on a regular basis, for example, quarterly reports to senior IT management and senior Customers to indicate the overall trends. Concentrating on areas where things have not been going as well as hoped for is required, but do not forget to report on the good news as well. It is vitally important that the reports show whether the CSIP has actually improved the overall service provision and if it has not, what actions will be taken to rectify the situation.

Consideration must also be given to the skills required to analyse the reports both from a technical viewpoint and from the viewpoint of interpreting results in terms of the business impact.

As well as using the tools to measure and report on the CSFs and KPIs the performance of the tool itself needs to be monitored to ensure it is supporting the people using it and the processes that have been developed.

6.1 Critical Success Factors and Key Performance Indicators

Critical Success Factors (CSFs) are the small number of things that have to be got right within each ITSM process. KPIs should be set and measured against each of the processes to ensure the CSFs are met. It should be noted that the characteristics of CSFs and KPIs are such that they cascade down from department to individual levels. Together, CSFs and KPIs establish the baseline and mechanisms for tracking performance.

It is recommended that each IT organisation focus on a small sub-set of CSFs and KPIs at any one instant. The required CSFs and KPIs should be set at the beginning of the CSIP.

6.1.1 Configuration Management

CSFs

- control of IT assets
- support the delivery of quality IT services
- economic service provision
- support, integration and interfacing to all other ITSM processes.

KPIs

Control of IT assets:

- percentage reduction in number of Configuration Item (CI) attribute errors found in Configuration Management Database (CMDB)
- percentage increase in the number of CIs successfully audited
- percentage improvements in the speed and accuracy of audit.

Support the delivery of quality IT services:

- percentage reduction in service errors attributable to wrong CI information
- improved speed of component repair and recovery
- improved Customer satisfaction with services and terminal equipment.

Economic service provision:

- reduction in the number of 'missing or duplicated' CIs

- greater percentage of maintenance costs and licence fees within budget
- percentage reduction in S/W costs due to better control
- percentage reduction in H/W costs due to better control of spares inventory and supplies
- percentage improvement in average cost of maintaining CIs in CMDB.

Support, integration and interfacing to all other ITSM processes:

- reduced percentage of Change failures as a result of inaccurate configuration data
- improved Incident resolution time due to the availability of complete and accurate configuration data
- more accurate results from Risk Analysis audits due to available and accurate asset information.

6.1.2   Change Management

CSFs

- a repeatable process for making Changes
- make Changes quickly and accurately (business driven needs)
- protect services when making Changes
- deliver process efficiency and effectiveness benefits.

KPIs

Repeatable process:

- percentage fewer rejected RFCs
- percentage reduction in unauthorised Changes detected
- percentage of Change requests (business driven need) implemented on time
- percentage reduction in average time to make Changes
- percentage reduction in the Change backlog
- percentage fewer Changes 'backed out' because of testing failures
- percentage reduction in Changes required by previous Change failures
- increase in the percentage of reports produced on schedule.

Quick and accurate Changes:

- percentage reduction in the number of urgent Changes
- percentage reduction of urgent Changes causing Incidents
- reduction in the percentage of Changes implemented without being tested
- percentage reduction of urgent Changes requiring back-out
- reduced percentage of urgent or high priority Changes submitted without business case to justify decision.

Protect service:

- reduction in both the scheduled and unscheduled service unavailability caused by Changes
- percentage reduction in Changes backed out
- percentage reduction of unsuccessful Changes
- percentage reduction in Changes causing Incidents
- percentage reduction in Changes impacting core service time and SLA service hours
- percentage increase in Changes activated outside core service time and SLA service hours
- reduction in the percentage of Changes not referred to a Change Advisory Board (CAB) or Change Advisory Board Emergency Committee (CAB/EC)
- improvement in Customer Satisfaction Survey (CSS) feedback on Change
- percentage reduction in failed Changes that do not have recorded back-out plan
- percentage reduction in time to implement a Change freeze.

Show efficiency and effectiveness results:

- percentage efficiency improvement based on number of RFCs processed
- percentage increase in the accuracy of Change estimates
- percentage reduction in the average cost of handling a Change
- percentage reduction in Change overtime due to better planning
- reduction in the 'cost' of failed Changes
- increased percentage of Changes implemented on time
- increased percentage of Changes implemented to budget
- reduction in the percentage of failed Changes
- reduction in the percentage of backed out Changes.

6.1.3   Release Management

CSFs

- better quality software and hardware
- a repeatable process for rolling out software and hardware Releases
- implementation of Releases swiftly (business driven needs) and accurately
- cost-effective releases.

KPIs

Better quality software and hardware:

- percentage reduction in the use of software and hardware Releases that have not passed the required quality checks
- percentage reduction in installed software not taken from DSL

- percentage reduction in non-standard hardware
- all bought-in software complies with legal restrictions
- percentage reduction of unauthorised reversion to previous Releases
- percentage reduction in the use of unauthorised software and hardware.

Repeatable process for rolling out software and hardware Releases:

- all new Releases planned and controlled by Release Management
- all installed software taken from the DSL
- all appropriate hardware stored in the DHS
- percentage reduction in the number of failed distributions of Releases to remote sites
- reduction in the percentage of urgent Releases
- increase in the percentage of 'normal Release units' as opposed to ad hoc Releases.

Implementation of Releases swiftly (business driven needs) and accurately:

- percentage reduction in build failures
- percentage implementation of releases at all sites, including remote ones, on time
- percentage reduction in the number of urgent Releases
- percentage reduction in the Releases causing Incidents
- reduction in the percentage of Releases implemented without being tested
- reduced percentage of urgent or high priority Releases requested without the appropriate business case/justification.

Cost-effective releases

- increased percentage of Releases built and implemented on schedule
- percentage Releases built and implemented within budget
- reduction in the service unavailability caused by Releases
- percentage reduction in Releases backed out
- percentage reduction of failed Releases
- percentage reduction in the average cost of handling a Release
- percentage reduction in Release overtime due to better planning
- reduction in the 'cost' of failed Releases
- no evidence of payment of licence fees or wasted maintenance effort, for software that is not in use
- no evidence of wasteful duplication in Release building (e.g. multiple builds of remote sites, when copies of a single build would suffice)
- percentage improvement of the planned composition of Releases matching the actual composition (which demonstrates good Release planning)
- percentage improvement in the resources required by Release Management
- percentage increase in the accuracy of Release estimates.

6.1.4 Incident Management

CSFs

- quickly resolve Incidents
- maintain IT service quality
- improve IT and business productivity
- maintain User satisfaction.

KPIs

Quickly resolve Incidents:

- percentage reduction in average time to respond to a call for assistance from first-line operatives
- percentage increase in the Incidents resolved by first line operatives
- percentage increase in the Incidents resolved by first line operatives on first response
- percentage reduction of Incidents incorrectly assigned
- percentage reduction of Incidents incorrectly categorised
- reduced mean elapsed time for resolution or circumvention of Incidents, broken down by impact code
- increased percentage of Incidents resolved within agreed (in SLAs) response times by impact code.

Maintain IT service quality:

- reduction in the service unavailability caused by Incidents
- increased percentage of Incidents resolved within target times by priority
- increased percentage of Incidents resolved within target times by category
- percentage reduction in the average time for second line support to respond
- reduction of the Incident backlog
- percentage increase in the Incidents fixed before Users notice
- percentage reduction in the Incidents reopened
- percentage reduction in the overall average time to resolve Incidents
- reduction in the number of Incidents requiring more than one second line support team.

Improve business and IT productivity:

- percentage reduction in average cost of handling incidents
- improve percentage of business incidents dealt with first line operatives
- percentage reduction number of times first line operatives bypassed
- percentage improvement in average number of incidents handled by each first line operatives

- no delays in the production of management reports
- improved scores on CSS responses.

User satisfaction:

- percentage improvement in CSS responses on the Incident Management service
- percentage reduction in length of queue time waiting for Service Desk response
- percentage reduction in the number of lost Service Desk calls
- percentage reduction of the number of revised business instructions issued.

6.1.5 Problem Management

CSFs

- improved service quality
- minimise impact of Problems
- reduce the cost to Users of Problems.

KPIs

Improve service quality:

- percentage reduction in repeat Incidents/Problems
- percentage reduction in the Incidents and Problems affecting service to Customers
- percentage reduction in the known Incidents and Problems encountered
- no delays in production of management reports
- improved CSS responses on business disruption caused by Incidents and Problems.

Minimise impact of Problems:

- percentage reduction in average time to resolve Problems
- percentage reduction of the time to implement fixes to Known Errors
- percentage reduction of the time to diagnose Problems
- percentage reduction of the average number of undiagnosed Problems
- percentage reduction of the average backlog of 'open' Problems and errors.

Reduction cost of Problems to Users:

- percentage reduction of the impact of Problems on User
- reduction in the business disruption caused by Incidents and Problems
- percentage reduction in the number of Problems escalated (missed target)
- percentage reduction in the IT Problem Management budget
- increased percentage of proactive Changes raised by Problem Management, particularly from Major Incident and Problem reviews.

6.1.6 Service Level Management

CSFs

- manage quantity and quality of IT services required
- deliver service as previously agreed
- provide services at affordable costs
- manage the interface with the business and Users.

KPIs

Manage quantity and quality of IT service needed:

- percentage reduction in SLA targets missed
- percentage reduction in SLA targets threatened
- percentage increase in Customer perception of SLA achievements via CSS responses
- percentage reduction in SLA breaches caused because of third party support contracts (Underpinning Contracts)
- percentage reduction in SLA breaches caused because of internal Operational Level Agreements (OLAs).

Deliver service as previously agreed at affordable costs:

- total number and percentage increase in fully documented SLAs in place
- percentage increase of SLAs agreed against operational services being run
- percentage increase in completeness of Service Catalogue versus operational services
- percentage improvement in the Service Delivery costs
- percentage reduction in the cost of monitoring and reporting of SLAs
- percentage increase in the speed and accuracy of developing SLAs.

Manage business interface:

- increased percentage of Services covered by SLAs
- documented and agreed SLM processes and procedures are in place
- reduction in the time to respond to and implement SLA requests
- increased percentage of SLA reviews completed on time
- reduction in the percentage of outstanding SLAs for annual renegotiation
- reduction in the percentage of SLAs requiring Changes (for example targets not attainable; Changes in usage levels)
- percentage increase in the number of OLAs and third Party contracts in place
- documentary evidence that issues raised at service and SLA reviews are being followed up and resolved (e.g. via the CSIP)?
- reduction in the number and severity of SLA breaches
- effective review and follow-up of all SLA, OLA and underpinning contract breaches.

6.1.7 Availability Management

CSFs

- manage availability and reliability of IT service
- satisfy business needs for access to IT services
- availability of IT infrastructure, as documented in SLAs, provided at optimum costs.

KPIs

Manage availability and reliability of IT service:

- percentage reduction in the unavailability of services and components
- percentage increase in the reliability of services and components
- effective review and follow-up of all SLA, OLA and underpinning contract breaches
- percentage improvement in overall end-to-end availability of services
- percentage reduction in the number and impact of service breaks
- improvement in the MTBF (mean time between failures)
- improvement in the MTBSI (mean time between system incidents)
- reduction in the MTTR (mean time to repair).

Satisfy business needs for access to IT services:

- percentage reduction in the unavailability of services
- percentage reduction of the cost of business overtime due to unavailable IT
- percentage reduction in critical time failures, e.g. specific business peak and priority availability needs are planned for
- percentage improvement in business and Users satisfied with service (by CSS results).

Availability of IT infrastructure achieved at optimum costs:

- percentage reduction in the cost of unavailability
- percentage improvement in the Service Delivery costs
- timely completion of regular risk analysis and system review
- timely completion of regular cost-benefit analysis established for infrastructure Component Failure Impact Analysis (CFIA)
- percentage reduction in failures of third party performance on MTTR/MTBF against contract targets
- reduced time taken to complete (or update) a risk analysis
- reduced time taken to review system resilience
- reduced time taken to complete an Availability Plan
- timely production of management reports
- percentage reduction in the incidence of operational reviews uncovering security and reliability exposures in application designs.

6.1.8   Capacity Management

CSFs

- accurate business forecasts
- knowledge of current and future technologies
- ability to demonstrate cost-effectiveness
- ability to plan and implement the appropriate IT capacity to match business need.

KPIs

Accurate business forecasts:

- production of workload forecasts on time
- percentage accuracy of forecasts of business trends
- timely incorporation of business plans into Capacity Plan
- reduction in the number of variances from the business plans and Capacity Plans.

Knowledge of current and future technologies:

- increased ability to monitor performance and throughput of all services and components
- timely justification and implementation of new technology in line with business requirements (time, cost and functionality)
- reduction in the use of old technology causing breached SLAs due to problems with support or performance.

Ability to demonstrate cost-effectiveness:

- a reduction in panic buying
- reduction in the over-capacity of IT
- accurate forecasts of planned expenditure
- reduction in the business disruption caused by a lack of adequate IT capacity
- relative reduction in the cost of production of the Capacity Plan.

Ability to plan and implement the appropriate IT capacity to match business needs:

- percentage reduction in the number of Incidents due to poor performance
- percentage reduction in lost business due to inadequate capacity
- all new services are implemented which match Service Level Requirements (SLRs)
- increased percentage of recommendations made by Capacity Management are acted upon
- reduction in the number of SLA breaches due to either poor service performance or poor component performance.

6.1.9   IT Service Continuity

CSFs

- IT Services are delivered and can be recovered to meet business objectives
- awareness throughout the organisation of the business and IT Service Continuity Plans.

KPIs

IT Services are delivered and can be recovered to meet business objectives:

- regular audits of the IT Service Continuity (ITSC) Plan to ensure that, at all times, the agreed recovery requirements of the business can be achieved
- all service recovery targets are agreed and documented in SLAs and are achievable within the IT Service Continuity Plan
- regular and comprehensive ITSC Plan testing
- regular reviews are undertaken, at least annually, of the business and IT Continuity plans with the business areas
- negotiate and manage all necessary ITSC contracts with third party
- overall reduction in the risk and impact of possible failure of IT services.

Awareness throughout the organisations of the plans:

- ensure awareness of business impact, needs and requirements throughout IT
- ensure that all IT Service areas and staff are prepared and able to respond to an invocation of the IT Service Continuity Plans.
- regular communication of the IT Service Continuity objectives and responsibilities within the appropriate business and IT Service areas.

6.1.10   IT Financial Management

CSFs

- effective stewardship of the IT finances
- overall effectiveness of the process
- Customers satisfied with costs and charges of services.

KPIs

Effective stewardship of the IT finances:

- increased accuracy of cost recovery profiles and expenditure
- the IT organisation is operated within the expected income/level of profits

- the IT financial objective of either break-even or profit (whichever is the objective of the enterprise) is met

- increased accuracy of monthly, quarterly and annual forecasted profiles

- reduced frequency and severity of Changes required to the Accounting and Budgeting systems

- all IT costs are accounted for

- reduced frequency and severity of Changes made to the Charging algorithms (where appropriate)

- timely production of budget forecasts and reports

- timely production of the Financial Plan, IT accounts and reports.

Overall effectiveness of the process:

- plans and budgets produced on time

- specified reports produced at the required time

- the inventory schedules are kept up-to-date

- timeliness of annual audits

- meeting of monthly, quarterly and annual financial objectives

- reduction in the relative costs

- reduction in the number of budget variances and adjustments

- reduction in the variances from the Financial Plan

- relative reduction in the overall Total Cost of Ownership (TCO).

Customers satisfied with cost of provision:

- charges, where applied, are seen to be fair

- reduction in the number queries and complaints from Customers relating to the calculation of IT costs and charges.

6.2 Organisational drivers

As outlined in Section 6.1, there are a number of KPIs for each of the ITSM processes that have to be monitored, collected and reported on. This should be performed within the steering framework, outlined in previous Chapters, of understanding the business drivers and ensuring that the CSIP is achieving the required results against these business drivers.

A recent survey conducted by *Computer Weekly* magazine asked Chief Executive Officers from large organisations, 'What do you want from IT services?' The top five responses were:

1 Support the business

2 Act as an agent for Change

3 Enable the business strategy

4 Lead the e-business capability

5 Facilitate business transformation.

Planning and implementing good ITSM processes can meet these requirements and it is important that these drivers are not forgotten throughout the CSIP.

Here are four examples of organisations that have completely different drivers for Change:

Example 1

A leading investment company decided to implement a major CSIP because they felt that cost savings could be made without impacting quality and because they felt that business case cost justification was not an integral part of the previous Change process. They needed to make the IT service provision more business and commercially focused. They conducted a fundamental organisational review with an emphasis initially on the people. They undertook an education programme concentrating on the cultural issues as well as ITIL processes. They then designed the new processes and purchased an integrated toolset to enable the processes to be performed effectively and efficiently. With trained staff, the right toolset and processes, they were able to improve service provision, reduce costs and, most importantly, they were able to show that this had occurred by defining appropriate, measurable, CSFs and KPIs.

Example 2

A leading network company was invited to tender for a major piece of work and within the Invitation To Tender (ITT) it stipulated that ITIL terminology and processes must be used. They therefore had to show in the proposal that they could work their processes within an ITIL framework. They had to show, by regular reports, that the ITIL processes were working well − at least as well as before they took over − and that they were on a path of continued improvement.

Example 3

A leading financial institution wanted to conduct a major business model transformation based on EFQM. The main focus was improvement in availability levels of their key IT processes that underpinned their major business processes. They needed to undertake major Organisation Change with clearly defined processes, people with defined roles and technology to support these two areas. They measured availability levels throughout to ensure that this was maintained throughout the CSIP and that the levels were improving at an acceptable rate for the business.

Example 4

A large British Central Government department decided that they wanted a leaner organisation. To achieve this they needed to undertake an organisational restructuring, moving lots of disparate groups into a more centralised structure. After an extensive analysis it was felt that the areas of Change Management, Incident Management and Problem Management were in the greatest need of improvement in terms of cost and quality. So they initially focused on Configuration Management (to enable the other processes to work more effectively), Change Management, Incident Management and Problem Management, all linked on a centralised integrated toolset. Again, it was important that they could show improvement throughout the process so the CSFs and KPIs were defined for these processes and reports regularly produced.

7 HOW DO WE KEEP THE MOMENTUM GOING?

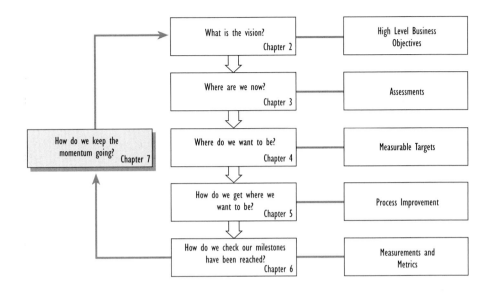

7.1 Overview

Anyone who has been on a diet can warn that the hardest part is keeping the weight off. The same is true for a CSIP – maintaining the improvements once they are achieved. Service Management is no different. There must be active attention paid to ongoing maintenance and further improvement to make sure that all the effort is not lost or forgotten, and to maximise learning and knowledge retention.

Sustaining improvement is made more complex by the fact that the rate of Change for IT operations continues to accelerate. This demand for Change is in direct response to the needs of business to adapt and innovate to stay competitive. ITIL processes support both the ability to incorporate Change quickly and to continuously assess and improve the overall operations environment. How and when these processes are implemented is completely dependent on the type and nature of the business and IT organisations using them, and the time, cost, and people available.

7.2 Consolidate Changes, produce more Change

As stated in Paragraph 5.3.7, use the success of quick wins to keep momentum going and to create more Change. In a CSIP, it is important to recognise short, middle and longer-term wins.

7.3 Institutionalise the Change

As stated in Paragraph 5.3.8, it is essential that major Changes be consolidated into everyday practice.

7.4   Ongoing monitoring and process reviews

For the purposes of this discussion, measuring is the process of gathering credible information or data in the CSIP areas. Monitoring is the repetition of this process at regular intervals, the accumulation of historical measuring results, and the analysis of this history for meaningful trends. These activities are complimentary and synergistic, with each adding value to the other. The four primary reasons to measure progress are to:

1   Determine progress toward goals and targets

2   Demonstrate effective use of business resources

3   Provide recognition, motivation, and feedback to team members, primary and extended

4   Allow action plans to be adjusted in consideration of actual results, and improve decision-making.

7.4.1   Progress towards goals and targets

Measures are a way to quantify what are often seen as subjective activities. The application of an objective measurement to the end goal and the current state helps the goal become more concrete and therefore able to be affected by action. The method of measurement and the yardstick should remain constant, so that progress can be gauged and tracked consistently and provide meaningful trend analysis.

7.4.2   Team recognition and motivation

Most new CSIPs meet with initial enthusiasm, which wanes over time as newer and more interesting initiatives arise. In order to keep the team and key advocates, sponsors, and participants motivated to remain engaged and focused on the process changes and key learning, they need to know they are making ongoing progress toward key goals and targets. Measuring and monitoring helps the team understand where they are, how far they've come, and where they need to go. It provides an opportunity for leadership to offer feedback on results and demonstrate support. It also makes it clear when significant milestones have been reached and when substantial barriers have been overcome.

7.4.3   Adjusting plans for results

Perhaps most important of all is what becomes of the measurement information once it has been gathered. The immediate purpose is to enable the team to review and understand results, and make adjustments as needed in moving forward. Short-term problems can be identified and addressed. Longer-term trends can also be identified and addressed before their impacts are too severe. Resources can be shifted as needed, and different approaches taken to future tasks if the team is adequately aware of their progress and problems to date.

7.4.4   Review of metrics

The essentials of measurement basics include time, costs, quality, and effectiveness. There are many valid approaches to measurement and Performance Management. Each organisation should determine what would be most effective for their situation. Measuring less than all major components may skew results and cause unintended impacts on the organisation. Selecting a balanced set of measures will help prevent this problem.

Measurements in these areas will address the following questions from team members, sponsors, and stakeholders:

- How effective are the metrics set?
- How is the work progressing against the metrics set?
- How well are stakeholders' expectations being met?
- How effective are the solutions provided in light of stakeholders' requirements?
- What are the costs to date?
- How do actual costs compare with budget?

Frequency of measurement is another consideration, and the ideal frequency may vary by situation or project. Strive to measure frequently enough to make necessary adjustments, but not so often as to create unnecessary work for the team. It is also appropriate to include relevant project results measurements in the development of employee performance appraisals, typically done once or twice a year. Because core team members are investing significant time and effort in the project, the project results should be considered in team members' personal effectiveness results. Including these contributions in performance reviews is also another way to provide recognition and motivation.

The best measurements are objective, credible, and require little downtime or overhead for the project team or others to compile. For these reasons, the use of automated tools to gather, report, and track measurements is encouraged whenever possible. Qualitative measures of effectiveness may be assisted somewhat by automated tools as well. To the extent that feedback from stakeholders and intended audiences can be gathered and reported electronically, this process will be quicker and easier. To whatever extent effectiveness and satisfaction rating can be numeric, the process will be further facilitated.

7.4.5   Ongoing quality improvement

The consolidation phase enables the organisation to take stock of what has been taking place and to ensure that improvements are embedded. Often, a series of improvements have been made to processes that require documentation (both to allow processes to be repeatable and to facilitate recognition of the achievement of some form of quality standard). For examples of TQM approaches, see Appendix I.

7.4.6   Auditing for improvement using key performance indicators

One common method of tracking metrics and trend analysis is through the use of a 'Balanced Scorecard'. The Balanced Scorecard is an aid to organisational Performance Management. It helps to focus, not only on the financial targets but also on the internal processes, Customers and learning and growth issues. The balance should be found between four perspectives.

The four perspectives are focused around the following questions:

1 Customers: what do our Customers desire?
2 Internal processes: how do we generate the added value for our Customers?

3 Learning and growth: how do we guarantee we will keep generating added value in the future?

4 Financial: how did we do financially?

The first three questions focus on the future, the last question reviews what has gone before. It is worthwhile discussing the Balanced Scorecard further at this point:

■ The Balanced Scorecard is not complex but to implement the scorecard successfully *is* complex. In practice, it can take an organisation up to three years to see the benefits of a Balanced Scorecard approach.

■ The Balanced Scorecard is not an exclusive IT feature. On the contrary, many organisations use scorecards in other departments – even at board level.

■ When implementing the Balanced Scorecard, it pays to start very conservatively. Start with three or four goals for each perspective. To do this, an organisation has to make choices; for many, this is extremely difficult and time consuming to do.

■ The most difficult part of using the Balanced Scorecard is not the implementation; it is the consolidation. Usually, consultants are employed to assist in the introduction of the Balanced Scorecard. The challenge is to keep measuring once they have gone.

■ The danger is in the temptation to fall back on prior measuring techniques or not measuring at all.

The Balanced Scorecard is complementary to ITIL. It is a way of measuring the effectiveness of the performance of the organisation. Some of the links include the following:

■ *client perspective:* this is relevant to most processes and is particularly relevant to Service Level Management where it is documented in Service Level Agreements

■ *internal processes:* these of course cover the ITIL processes

■ *learning and growth:* refers to staffing, training and investments in software

■ *financial:* IT Financial Management covers the way costs are allocated to the Customer organisation.

Once the objectives have been selected within each of the four perspective areas, the appropriate KPIs and CSFs should be selected to consider the progression towards achievement of these objectives.

Another auditing method, COBIT, is discussed in Paragraph 3.9.3.

7.5 Reinforce business and IT alignment continuously

IT industry analyst reviews have raised a number of consistent themes on the importance of IT value to the business goals, and the challenges associated with this:

■ IT performance is now being measured on business results

■ IT continues to struggle to measure its real value to the business

■ IT wants to reorient its attention towards business issues as expressed in IT infrastructure and processes

■ relating the complex interaction of systems, networks, applications, services, and business processes is difficult with current Service Management tools.

Work will be of higher quality, and in the right order of importance, when the business priorities make it clear how operations affect the business, and which parts are affected in what ways. This must be linked to the IT maturity level of the organisation. Developing new systems and maintaining existing systems while responding to changing business priorities can be a difficult challenge, but it is a basic premise of every IT culture. Additionally, personal job satisfaction and pride come from understanding the business vision and how each individual can contribute to achieving the company's business priorities.

7.6 Knowledge Management

Conducting business in today's market is vastly different from what it was 10 years ago. Just in that short amount of time there has been:

- an increase in the rate of change in industry and market landscapes, as barriers to entry have decreased and new opportunities opened up

- an increase in employee turnover, as it has become more socially acceptable and often beneficial to change companies during a career to develop and share new experiences and perspectives

- an increase in access to information via the Internet and a more open global economy

- bigger market competition forcing company employees to share knowledge between departments and subsidiaries.

7.6.1 Knowledge Management concepts

Effective Knowledge Management enables a company to optimise the benefits of these Changes, while at the same time:

- enhancing its organisation's effectiveness through better decision-making enabled by having the right information at the right time, and facilitating enterprise learning through the exchange and development of ideas and individuals

- enhancing Customer/Supplier relationships through sharing information and services to expand capabilities through collaborative efforts

- improving business processes through sharing lessons learned, results, and best practices across the organisation.

Knowledge Management is key to an enterprise's viability, from capturing the competitive advantage in an industry to decreasing cycle time and cost of an IT implementation. How to cultivate the knowledge depends heavily on the make-up of the existing knowledge base, and Knowledge Management norms for cultural interaction.

There are two main components to successful Knowledge Management:

1 An open culture, where knowledge, both best practices and lessons learned, is shared across the organisation and individuals are rewarded for it. Many cultures foster an environment where 'knowledge is power' (the more you know that others do not, the more valuable you are to the company). This type of knowledge hoarding is a dangerous behaviour for a company to reward, since demand for the knowledge may easily outweigh supply, causing unnecessary slow-down in progress, and in such a high turnover industry as IT, that knowledge may leave the company at any time,

potentially leaving the company with a crippling deficiency. Another tenet of an open culture is a willingness to learn. This is an environment where growing an individual's knowledge base is rewarded and facilitated through open support and opportunities.

2 The infrastructure – a culture may be open to knowledge sharing, but without the means or infrastructure to support it, even the best intentions can be impaired, and over time this serves as a demotivator, quelling the behaviour. This infrastructure can be defined in various ways, it may be a technical application or system which allows individuals to conduct on-line, self-paced training, or it may be a process such as post-mortems or knowledge sharing activities designed to bring people together to discuss best practices or lessons learned.

The identification of knowledge gaps and resulting sharing and development of that knowledge must be built into the process throughout the IT lifecycle. This also raises the issues of dependencies and priorities. Knowledge on how to build and deploy the IT solution will be needed before the knowledge to operate the solution will be applied. So the IT lifecycle itself drives a natural priority of knowledge development and sharing. But regardless of what area in the lifecycle of an IT project an organisation is dealing with, it is important to identify and develop the necessary knowledge base prior to the moment where the knowledge may be applied. This may seem obvious and yet the majority of organisations fail to recognise the need and train the individuals until the process is halted due to a skills shortage. Knowledge sharing is an activity that should be fostered prior to, during and after the application of knowledge to the task.

It should be noted that Knowledge Management could be seen at the opposite end of a spectrum of fully automated processes that have all the required knowledge built into the process itself. Service Management processes fall somewhere between these two extremes, with the operational processes nearer to the automation of processes than the tactical or strategic processes. This should be taken into account when designing the processes as Knowledge Management viewpoints may very well enable quick wins on the more Knowledge Management intensive processes. This is not to imply that there would be a difference of levels of knowledge required for the people participating to the processes – rather that, in order to further develop SLM and vendor-management processes, the tacit knowledge needs to be harvested. It is easier to automate the operational level processes than the tactical or strategic processes, which require a greater breadth and depth of knowledge.

Throughout a CSIP, a lot of experience and information is acquired. It is important that this knowledge be gathered, organised and accessible. To ensure the ongoing success of the programme, Knowledge Management techniques must be applied.

8 SUMMARY

Planning and implementation of Service Management is about assessing what needs to be done and then producing a plan to do it. The improvements can be based around the processes of ITSM, around the technology that supports the processes, or around the people who operate the processes. The main driver for improvement, however, will come from the business needs and the business priorities. It may be that the organisation cannot justify immediately wholesale implementation, so addressing the areas of greatest need now and planning the longer-term strategies for the future will be required. The CSIP must, in an integrated way, address people, process, technology and business steering. It is important that a strategy is produced that identifies short, medium and long-term improvements to Service Delivery and Service Support.

The implementation of Service Management is not a one-off project but rather a continuous process of service improvement. There is a need to continuously understand where improvements are required to ensure the service provision is maintained at a high standard. There will be a need for active and ongoing staff commitment especially from senior management.

There will be issues, as discussed earlier in the book, which will arise throughout the CSIP. These issues have to be recognised and addressed and if possible they should be prevented. Inevitably any change to the way of working will be met by denial, or at least a resistance to change, by some members of staff. Good communications and involvement in the CSIP are key to gaining wide support. The IT organisation must be focused on the overall strategy and understand that knowledge and membership of Service Management is part of everyone's everyday job. Therefore it is vital that everyone understands this Service Management strategy and the CSIP.

An important element of planning, implementing and ongoing maintenance of IT Service Management is focused reporting and statistical analysis to ensure the changes are having the desired effect. It is important that where changes to the way of working are not having the desired effect, the programme is amended. It is also equally important that where improvements have been achieved, these are communicated to IT staff as well as Users and Customers of the IT services.

This book refers to the need for assessing and planning. It is imperative that these tasks are undertaken – however, it is equally important that something is done. Often, organisations spend too long assessing and planning and then reassessing without actually taking any action to improve service quality. So when the improvement plan has been produced, it is important to take action to achieve the objectives.

This book details ways to implement improvement initiatives to the quality of IT Service Provision. Doing this will help to improve the chances of business success, and give IT staff the opportunity of playing a key role in supporting the overall business vision.

9 BIBLIOGRAPHY

Note: that the entries in this Bibliography are given throughout in alphabetical order of title within each Section.

9.1 References

Acquisition
OGC IS Management Guide, www.ogc.gov.uk Tel: +44(0) 845 000 4999
Published by Format
ISBN 1 90309 1 03 9

The Balanced Scorecard: Translating Strategy into Action
Robert S. Kaplan, David P. Norton 1996
Published by Harvard Business School Press, Boston, MA
ISBN: 0 87584 651-3

Code of Practice for IT Service Management (A), DISC PD0005
Extracts are reproduced with the permission of BSI under licence number PD\ 1999 0877. Complete copies of the standard can be obtained by post from BSI Customer Services, 389 Chiswick High Road, London W4 4AL
www.bsi.ork.uk/disc/products, Tel: 020 8996 9001

The Cultures of Work Organisations
Trice/Beyer 1993
Published by Prentice Hall, NJ.
ISBN 0 13 191438 3

In Search of Excellence: Lessons From America's Best Run Companies
Thomas Peters, Robert H. Waterman, Tom Peters 1995
Published by Harper Collins
ISBN 0 00 638402 1

Leading Change
John P. Kotter 1996
Published by Harvard Business School Press, Boston, MA
ISBN: 0 875847 47 1

Management System for the Information Business (A)
IBM

A Management System for the Information Business: Organisational Analysis
Edward A Van Shaik

Managing Change
OGC IS Management Guide, www.ogc.gov.uk Tel: +44(0) 845 000 4999
Published by Format 1999
ISBN 1 90309 1 01 2

Managing the Data Resource Function
Richard Nolan

Managing Performance
OGC IS Management Guide, www.ogc.gov.uk Tel: +44(0) 845 000 4999
Published by Format 1999
ISBN 1 90309 1 05 5

Managing Services
OGC IS Management Guide, www.ogc.gov.uk Tel: +44(0) 845 000 4999
Published by Format 1999
ISBN 1 90309 1 04 7

Managing Successful Projects with PRINCE2
Published by The Stationery Office, London 1999
Available from OGC, www.ogc.gov.uk Tel: +44(0) 845 000 4999 or The Stationery Office,
tel. 0870 600 5522
ISBN 0 11 330855 8

PRINCE2 Project Management for Business
Publishd by The Stationery Office, London
Available from OGC, www.ogc.gov.uk Tel: +44(0) 845 000 4999 or The Stationery Office,
tel. 0870 600 5522
ISBN 0 11 330685 7

Process Innovation
Thomas H Davenport 1993
Published by HBS, Boston, MA
ISBN 0 87584 366 2

Quantitative Assessment of Maintenance, An Industrial Case Study
H.D. Rombach, V.R. Basili

Re-organisational Transformations
Raul Espejo, Werner Schumann, Markus Schwaninger, Ubaldo Bilello 1996
Published by John Wiley and Sons; Chichester, UK
ISBN 0 471 968182 5

Proceedings of Conference on Software Maintenance, Austin, Texas, U.S.A., pp.135 144. 1987.

Service Quality
Brown, Gummesson, Edvardsson, Gustavsson 1991
Published by Lexington Books; N.Y., U.S.A.
ISBN 0 669 21152 4

Six Sigma: The Breakthrough Management Strategy: Revolutionizing the World's Top Corporations
Mike J. Harry, Richard Schroeder 1999
Published by Bantam Doubleday Dell Books
ISBN 0 38 549437 8

Specification for IT Service Management, BSI5000
Complete copies of the standard can be obtained by post from BSI Customer Services, 389
Chiswick High Road, London W4 4AL
www.bsi.ork.uk/disc/products Tel: 020-8996 9001

Strategic Management of IS
OGC IS Management Guide, www.ogc.gov.uk Tel: +44(0) 845 000 4999
Published by Format
ISBN 1 90309 1 02 0

Structures in Fives: Designing Effective Organisations
Minzberg 1993
Published by Prentice Hall, NJ
ISBN 0 13 855479 X

What is This Thing Called Theory of Constraints and How it Should be Implemented
Eliyahu M. Goldratt 1999
Published by North River Press
ISBN 0 88 427166 8

9.2   Other Sources

British Standards Institution
Website at www.bsi.org.uk

CMM
Website at www.sei.cmu.edu/cmm

European Foundation for Quality Management
Website at www.efqm.org '...the battle for Quality is one of the prerequisites for the success of
your companies and for our collective success'.
Jacques Delors

ISO 9000 Information Forum
Website at www.iso 9000.co.uk

Office of Government Commerce (OGC)
Website at www.ogc.gov.uk

W. Edwards Deming Institute (The)
Website at www.deming.org. 'We should work on our process, not the outcome of our processes.'
W. Edwards Deming

APPENDIX A LIST OF ACRONYMS AND GLOSSARY

A.1 Acronyms

AMDB	Availability Management Database
ARCI	Accountability, Responsibility, Consulted, Informed
BIA	Business Impact Analysis
BPR	Business Process Re engineering
BSI	British Standards Institute
CAB	Change Advisory Board
CAB/EC	Change Advisory Board Emergency Committee
CBT	Computer Based Training
CDB	Capacity (Management) Database
CFIA	Component Failure Impact Analysis
CI	Configuration Item
CIO	Chief Information Officer
CMDB	Configuration Management Database
CMM	Capability Maturity Model
COBIT	Control Objectives for Information and Related Technology
CSF	Critical Success Factor
CSIP	Continuous Service Improvement Programme
CSS	Customer Satisfaction Survey
CTO	Chief Technology Officer
DSL	Definitive Software Library
EFQM	European Foundation for Quality Management
EXIN	Examination Institute for Information Science
ICT	Information and Communication Technology
ICTSG	ICT Steering Group
ISEB	Information Systems Examination Board
ISG	IT Steering Group
ISO	International Standards Organisation

IT	Information Technology
ITIL	Information Technology Infrastructure Library
ITSC	IT Service Continuity
ITSM	Information Technology Service Management
*it*SMF	IT Service Management Forum
IVR	Interactive Voice Response
KPI	Key Performance Indicator
MAC	Movements, Additions and Changes
MTBF	Mean Time Between Failures
MTBSI	Mean Time Between System Incidents
MTTR	Mean Time To Repair
OGC	Office of Government Commerce
OLA	Operational Level Agreement
PIR	Post Implementation Review
PMF	Process Maturity Framework
R and D	Research and Development
RFC	Request For Change
SEI	Software Engineering Institute
SLA	Service Level Agreement
SLM	Service Level Management
SLR	Service Level Requirement
SMART	Specific, Measurable, Achievable, Realistic, Time related
SOCITM	Society of Council IT Managers
SOR	Statement Of Requirements
SPI	Software Process Improvement
SPICE	Software Process Improvement and Capability dEtermination
SPMF	Service management Process Maturity Framework
SWOT	Strengths, Weaknesses, Opportunities and Threats
TCO	Total Cost of Ownership
TQM	Total Quality Management
TTO	Transfer To Operation
WORM	Write Once, Read Many (optical read only disks)

A.2 Glossary

absorbed overhead

> Overhead which, by means of absorption rates, is included in costs of specific products or saleable services, in a given period of time. Under or over absorbed overhead. The difference between overhead cost incurred and overhead cost absorbed: it may be split into its two constituent parts for control purposes.

absorption costing

> A principle whereby fixed as well as variable costs are allotted to cost units and total overheads are absorbed according to activity level. The term may be applied where production costs only, or costs of all functions are so allotted.

action lists

> Defined actions, allocated to recovery teams and individuals, within a phase of a plan. These are supported by reference data.

alert

> Warning that an incident has occurred.

alert phase

> The first phase of a business continuity plan in which initial emergency procedures and damage assessments are activated.

allocated cost

> A cost that can be directly identified with a business unit.

apportioned cost

> A cost that is shared by a number of business units (an indirect cost). This cost must be shared out between these units on an equitable basis.

asset

> Component of a business process. Assets can include people, accommodation, computer systems, networks, paper records, fax machines, etc.

asynchronous/synchronous

> In a communications sense, the ability to transmit each character as a self contained unit of information, without additional timing information. This method of transmitting data is sometimes called start/stop. Synchronous working involves the use of timing information to allow transmission of data, which is normally done in blocks. Synchronous transmission is usually more efficient than the asynchronous method.

availability

> Ability of a component or service to perform its required function at a stated instant or over a stated period of time. It is usually expressed as the availability ratio, i.e. the proportion of time that the service is actually available for use by the Customers within the agreed service hours.

Balanced Scorecard

> An aid to organisational Performance Management. It helps to focus, not only on the financial targets but also on the internal processes, Customers, and learning and growth issues.

baseline

A snapshot or a position that is recorded. Although the position may be updated later, the baseline remains unchanged and available as a reference of the original state and as a comparison against the current position (PRINCE2).

baseline security

The security level adopted by the IT organisation for its own security and from the point of view of good 'due diligence'.

baselining

Process by which the quality and cost effectiveness of a service is assessed, usually in advance of a change to the service. Baselining usually includes comparison of the service before and after the change or analysis of trend information. The term benchmarking is usually used if the comparison is made against other enterprises.

bridge

Equipment and techniques used to match circuits to each other ensuring minimum transmission impairment.

BS7799

The British Standard for Information Security Management. This standard provides a comprehensive set of controls comprising best practices in information security.

budgeting

Budgeting is the process of predicting and controlling the spending of money within the organisation and consists of a periodic negotiation cycle to set budgets (usually annual) and the day to day monitoring of current budgets.

build

The final stage in producing a usable configuration. The process involves taking one or more input Configuration Items and processing them (building them) to create one or more output Configuration Items, e.g. software compile and load.

business function

A business unit within an organisation, e.g. a department, division, branch.

business process

A group of business activities undertaken by an organisation in pursuit of a common goal. Typical business processes include receiving orders, marketing services, selling products, delivering services, distributing products, invoicing for services, accounting for money received. A business process usually depends upon several business functions for support, e.g. IT, personnel, accommodation. A business process rarely operates in isolation, i.e. other business processes will depend on it and it will depend on other processes.

business recovery objective

The desired time within which business processes should be recovered, and the minimum staff, assets and services required within this time.

business recovery plan framework

A template business recovery plan (or set of plans) produced to allow the structure and proposed contents to be agreed before the detailed business recovery plan is produced.

business recovery plans

Documents describing the roles, responsibilities and actions necessary to resume business processes following a business disruption.

business recovery team

A defined group of personnel with a defined role and subordinate range of actions to facilitate recovery of a business function or process.

business unit

A segment of the business entity by which both revenues are received and expenditure are caused or controlled, such revenues and expenditure being used to evaluate segmental performance.

Capital Costs

Typically those costs applying to the physical (substantial) assets of the organisation. Traditionally this was the accommodation and machinery necessary to produce the enterprise's product. Capital Costs are the purchase or major enhancement of fixed assets, for example computer equipment (building and plant) and are often also referred to as 'one off' costs.

capital investment appraisal

The process of evaluating proposed investment in specific fixed assets and the benefits to be obtained from their acquisition. The techniques used in the evaluation can be summarised as non discounting methods (i.e. simple pay back), return on capital employed and discounted cashflow methods (i.e. yield, net present value and discounted pay back).

capitalisation

The process of identifying major expenditure as Capital, whether there is a substantial asset or not, to reduce the impact on the current financial year of such expenditure. The most common item for this to be applied to is software, whether developed in house or purchased.

category

Classification of a group of Configuration Items, Change documents or problems.

Change

The addition, modification or removal of approved, supported or baselined hardware, network, software, application, environment, system, desktop build or associated documentation.

Change Advisory Board (CAB)

A group of people who can give expert advice to Change Management on the implementation of Changes. This board is likely to be made up of representatives from all areas within IT and representatives from business units.

Change Authority

A group that is given the authority to approve Change, e.g. by the project board. Sometimes referred to as the Configuration Board.

Change Control

The procedure to ensure that all Changes are controlled, including the submission, analysis, decision making, approval, implementation and post-implementation of the Change.

Change document

> Request for Change, Change control form, Change order, Change record.

Change history

> Auditable information that records, for example, what was done, when, who did it, and why.

Change log

> A log of Requests for Change raised during the project, showing information on each Change, its evaluation what decisions have been made and its current status, e.g. Raised, Reviewed, Approved, Implemented, Closed.

Change Management

> Process of controlling Changes to the infrastructure or any aspect of services, in a controlled manner, enabling approved Changes with minimum disruption.

Change record

> A record containing details of which CIs are affected by an authorised Change (planned or implemented) and how.

charging

> The process of establishing charges in respect of business units, and raising the relevant invoices for recovery from Customers.

classification

> Process of formally grouping Configuration Items by type, e.g. software, hardware, documentation, environment, application.
>
> Process of formally identifying Changes by type e.g. project scope change request, validation change request, infrastructure change request.
>
> Process of formally identifying incidents, problems and known errors by origin, symptoms and cause.

closure

> When the Customer is satisfied that an incident has been resolved.

cold stand by

> See 'gradual recovery'.

command, control and communications

> The processes by which an organisation retains overall coordination of its recovery effort during invocation of business recovery plans.

Computer Aided Systems Engineering (CASE)

> A software tool for programmers. It provides help in the planning, analysis, design and documentation of computer software.

Configuration baseline

> Configuration of a product or system established at a specific point in time, which captures both the structure and details of the product or system, and enables that product or system to be rebuilt at a later date.
>
> A snapshot or a position that is recorded. Although the position may be updated later, the baseline remains unchanged and available as a reference of the original state and as a comparison against the current position (PRINCE2).

See also 'baseline'.

Configuration control

Activities comprising the control of Changes to Configuration Items after formally establishing its configuration documents. It includes the evaluation, coordination, approval or rejection of Changes. The implementation of Changes includes changes, deviations and waivers that impact on the configuration.

Configuration documentation

Documents that define requirements, system design, build, production, and verification for a configuration item.

Configuration identification

Activities that determine the product structure, the selection of Configuration Items, and the documentation of the Configuration Items' physical and functional characteristics, including interfaces and subsequent Changes. It includes the allocation of identification characters or numbers to the Configuration Items and their documents. It also includes the unique numbering of configuration control forms associated with Changes and Problems.

Configuration Item (CI)

Component of an infrastructure – or an item, such as a Request for Change, associated with an infrastructure – which is (or is to be) under the control of Configuration Management. CIs may vary widely in complexity, size and type – from an entire system (including all hardware, software and documentation) to a single module or a minor hardware component.

Configuration Management

The process of identifying and defining the Configuration Items in a system, recording and reporting the status of Configuration Items and Requests for Change, and verifying the completeness and correctness of configuration items.

Configuration Management Database (CMDB)

A database that contains all relevant details of each CI and details of the important relationships between CIs.

Configuration Management plan

Document setting out the organisation and procedures for the Configuration Management of a specific product, project, system, support group or service.

Configuration Management Tool (CM Tool)

A software product providing automatic support for Change, Configuration or version control.

Configuration Structure

A hierarchy of all the CIs that comprise a configuration.

Contingency Planning

Planning to address unwanted occurrences that may happen at a later time. Traditionally, the term has been used to refer to planning for the recovery of IT systems rather than entire business processes.

Continuous Service Improvement Programme

An ongoing formal programme undertaken within an organisation to identify and introduce measurable improvements within a specified work area or work process.

cost

The amount of expenditure (actual or notional) incurred on, or attributable to, a specific activity or business unit.

cost effectiveness

Ensuring that there is a proper balance between the quality of service on the one side and expenditure on the other. Any investment that increases the costs of providing IT services should always result in enhancement to service quality or quantity.

cost management

All the procedures, tasks and deliverables that are needed to fulfil an organisation's costing and charging requirements.

cost of failure

A technique used to evaluate and measure the cost of failed actions and activities. It can be measured as a total within a period or an average per failure. An example would be 'the cost of failed changes per month' or 'the average cost of a failed change'

cost unit

In the context of CSBC the cost unit is a functional cost unit which establishes standard cost per workload element of activity, based on calculated activity ratios converted to cost ratios.

costing

The process of identifying the costs of the business and of breaking them down and relating them to the various activities of the organisation.

countermeasure

A check or restraint on the service designed to enhance security by reducing the risk of an attack (by reducing either the threat or the vulnerability), reducing the Impact of an attack, detecting the occurrence of an attack and/or assisting in the recovery from an attack.

crisis management

The processes by which an organisation manages the wider impact of a disaster, such as adverse media coverage.

Critical Success Factor

A measure of success or maturity of a project or process. It can be a state, a deliverable or a milestone. An example of a CSF would be 'the production of an overall technology strategy'.

Customer

Recipient of the service; usually the Customer management has responsibility for the cost of the service, either directly through charging or indirectly in terms of demonstrable business need.

data transfer time

The length of time taken for a block or sector of data to be read from or written to an I/O device, such as a disk or tape.

Definitive Software Library (DSL)

The library in which the definitive authorised versions of all software CIs are stored and protected. It is a physical library or storage repository where master copies of software versions are placed. This one logical storage area may in reality consist of one or more physical software libraries or filestores. They should be separate from development and test filestore areas. The DSL may also include a physical store to hold master copies of bought in software, e.g. fireproof safe. Only authorised software should be accepted into the DSL, strictly controlled by Change Management and Release Management.

The DSL exists not directly because of the needs of the Configuration Management process, but as a common base for the Release Management and Configuration Management processes.

Delta Release

A Delta, or partial, Release is one that includes only those CIs within the Release unit that have actually changed or are new since the last full or Delta Release. For example, if the Release unit is the program, a Delta Release contains only those modules that have changed, or are new, since the last full release of the program or the last Delta Release of the modules.

See also 'Full Release'.

dependency

The reliance, either direct or indirect, of one process or activity upon another.

depreciation

The loss in value of an asset due to its use and/or the passage of time. The annual depreciation charge in accounts represents the amount of capital assets used up in the accounting period. It is charged in the cost accounts to ensure that the cost of capital equipment is reflected in the unit costs of the services provided using the equipment. There are various methods of calculating depreciation for the period, but the Treasury usually recommends the use of current cost asset valuation as the basis for the depreciation charge.

differential charging

Charging business Customers different rates for the same work, typically to dampen demand or to generate revenue for spare capacity. This can also be used to encourage off peak or night time running.

direct cost

A cost that is incurred for, and can be traced in full to a product, service, cost centre or department. This is an allocated cost. Direct costs are direct materials, direct wages and direct expenses.

See also 'indirect cost'.

disaster recovery planning

A series of processes that focus only upon the recovery processes, principally in response to physical disasters, which are contained within BCM.

discounted cashflow

An evaluation of the future net cashflows generated by a capital project by discounting them to their present day value. The two methods most commonly used are:

- yield method, for which the calculation determines the internal rate of return (IRR) in the form of a percentage

- net present value (NPV) method, in which the discount rate is chosen and the answer is a sum of money.

discounting

The offering to business Customers of reduced rates for the use of off peak resources.

See also 'surcharging'.

disk cache controller

Memory that is used to store blocks of data that have been read from the disk devices connected to them. If a subsequent I/O requires a record that is still resident in the cache memory, it will be picked up from there, thus saving another physical I/O.

downtime

Total period that a service or component is not operational, within an agreed service times.

duplex (full and half)

Full duplex line/channel allows simultaneous transmission in both directions. Half duplex line/channel is capable of transmitting in both directions, but only in one direction at a time.

echoing

A reflection of the transmitted signal from the receiving end, a visual method of error detection in which the signal from the originating device is looped back to that device so that it can be displayed.

elements of cost

The constituent parts of costs according to the factors upon which expenditure is incurred viz., materials, labour and expenses.

End User

See 'User'.

environment

A collection of hardware, software, network communications and procedures that work together to provide a discrete type of computer service. There may be one or more environments on a physical platform e.g. test, production. An environment has unique features and characteristics that dictate how they are administered in similar, yet diverse manners.

Expert User

See 'Super User'.

external target

One of the measures, against which a delivered IT service is compared, expressed in terms of the Customer's business.

financial year

An accounting period covering 12 consecutive months. In the public sector this financial year generally coincides with the fiscal year, which runs from 1 April to 31 March.

first line support

Help Desk call logging and resolution (on agreed areas, for example, MS Word).

first time fix rate

Commonly used metric, used to define incidents resolved at the first point of contact between a Customer and the service provider, without delay or referral, generally by a front line support group such as a help desk or service desk. First time fixes are a sub set of remote fixes.

Forward Schedule of Changes (FSC)

Contains details of all the Changes approved for implementation and their proposed implementation dates. It should be agreed with the Customers and the business, Service Level Management, the Service Desk and Availability Management. Once agreed, the Service Desk should communicate to the User community at large any planned additional downtime arising from implementing the Changes, using the most effective methods available.

full cost

The total cost of all the resources used in supplying a service i.e. the sum of the direct costs of producing the output, a proportional share of overhead costs and any selling and distribution expenses. Both cash costs and notional (non cash) costs should be included, including the cost of capital.

See also 'Total Cost of Ownership'.

Full Release

All components of the Release unit are built, tested, distributed and implemented together.

See also 'Delta Release'.

Gateway

Equipment that is used to interface networks so that a terminal on one network can communicate with services or a terminal on another.

gradual recovery

Previously called 'Cold stand by', this is applicable to organisations that do not need immediate restoration of business processes and can function for a period of up to 72 hours, or longer, without a re establishment of full IT facilities. This may include the provision of empty accommodation fully equipped with power, environmental controls and local network cabling infrastructure, telecommunications connections, and available in a disaster situation for an organisation to install its own computer equipment.

hard charging

Descriptive of a situation where, within an organisation, actual funds are transferred from the Customer to the IT organisation in payment for the delivery of IT services.

hard fault

The situation in a virtual memory system when the required page of code or data, which a program was using, has been redeployed by the operating system for some other purpose. This means that another piece of memory must be found to accommodate the code or data, and will involve physical reading/writing of pages to the page file.

host

A host computer comprises the central hardware and software resources of a computer complex, e.g. CPU, memory, channels, disk and magnetic tape I/O subsystems plus operating and applications software. The term is used to denote all non network items.

hot stand by

See 'immediate recovery'.

ICT

The convergence of Information Technology, Telecommunications and Data Networking Technologies into a single technology.

immediate recovery

Previously called 'hot stand by', provides for the immediate restoration of services following any irrecoverable incident. It is important to distinguish between the previous definition of 'hot stand by' and 'immediate recovery'. Hot stand by typically referred to availability of services within a short timescale such as 2 or 4 hours whereas immediate recovery implies the instant availability of services.

impact

Measure of the business criticality of an Incident. Often equal to the extent to which an Incident leads to distortion of agreed or expected service levels.

impact analysis

The identification of critical business processes, and the potential damage or loss that may be caused to the organisation resulting from a disruption to those processes. Business impact analysis identifies:

- the form the loss or damage will take

- how that degree of damage or loss is likely to escalate with time following an incident

- the minimum staffing, facilities and services needed to enable business processes to continue to operate at a minimum acceptable level

- the time within which they should be recovered.

The time within which full recovery of the business processes is to be achieved is also identified.

impact code

Simple code assigned to incidents and problems, reflecting the degree of impact upon the Customer's business processes. It is the major means of assigning priority for dealing with incidents.

impact scenario

Description of the type of impact on the business that could follow a business disruption. Usually related to a business process and will always refer to a period of time, e.g. Customer services will be unable to operate for two days.

Incident

Any event which is not part of the standard operation of a service and which causes, or may cause, an interruption to, or a reduction in, the quality of that service.

Incident Control

> The process of identifying, recording, classifying and progressing incidents until affected services return to normal operation.

indirect cost

> A cost incurred in the course of making a product providing a service or running a cost centre or department, but which cannot be traced directly and in full to the product, service or department, because it has been incurred for a number of cost centres or cost units. These costs are apportioned to cost centres/cost units. Indirect costs are also referred to as overheads.

> See also 'direct cost'.

Informed Customer

> An individual, team or group with functional responsibility within an organisation for ensuring that spend on IS/IT is directed to best effect, i.e. that the business is receiving value for money and continues to achieve the most beneficial outcome. In order to fulfil its role the 'Informed' Customer function must gain clarity of vision in relation to the business plans and assure that suitable strategies are devised and maintained for achieving business goals.

> The 'Informed' Customer function ensures that the needs of the business are effectively translated into a business requirements specification, that IT investment is both efficiently and economically directed, and that progress towards effective business solutions is monitored. The 'Informed' Customer should play an active role in the procurement process, e.g. in relation to business case development, and also in ensuring that the services and solutions obtained are used effectively within the organisation to achieve maximum business benefits. The term is often used in relation to the outsourcing of IT/IS. Sometimes also called 'Intelligent Customer'.

interface

> Physical or functional interaction at the boundary between Configuration Items.

intermediate recovery

> Previously called 'warm stand by', typically involves the re establishment of the critical systems and services within a 24 to 72 hour period, and is used by organisations that need to recover IT facilities within a predetermined time to prevent impacts to the business process.

internal target

> One of the measures against which supporting processes for the IT service are compared. Usually expressed in technical terms relating directly to the underpinning service being measured.

invocation (of business recovery plans)

> Putting business recovery plans into operation after a business disruption.

invocation (of stand by arrangements)

> Putting stand by arrangements into operation as part of business recovery activities.

invocation and recovery phase

> The second phase of a business recovery plan.

ISO 9001

The internationally accepted set of standards concerning Quality Management systems.

IT accounting

The set of processes that enable the IT organisation to account fully for the way money is spent (particularly the ability to identify costs by Customer, by service and by activity).

IT directorate

The part of an organisation charged with developing and delivering the IT services.

IT Infrastructure

The sum of an organisation's IT related hardware, software, data telecommunication facilities, procedures and documentation.

IT service

A described set of facilities, IT and non IT, supported by the IT service provider that fulfils one or more needs of the Customer and that is perceived by the Customer as a coherent whole.

IT service provider

The role of IT service provider is performed by any organisational units, whether internal or external, that deliver and support IT services to a Customer.

ITIL

The OGC IT Infrastructure Library – a set of guides on the management and provision of operational IT services.

Key Performance Indicator

A measurable quantity against which specific performance criteria can be set when drawing up the SLA.

Key Success Indicator

A measurement of success or maturity of a project or process.

See also 'Critical Success Factor'.

Known Error

An Incident or Problem for which the root cause is known and for which a temporary Work-around or a permanent alternative has been identified. If a business case exists, an RFC will be raised, but, in any event, it remains a Known Error unless it is permanently fixed by a Change.

latency

The elapsed time from the moment when a seek was completed on a disk device to the point when the required data is positioned under the read/write heads. It is normally defined by manufacturers as being half the disk rotation time.

lifecycle

A series of states, connected by allowable transitions. The lifecycle represents an approval process for Configuration Items, Problem Reports and Change documents.

logical I/O

> A read or write request by a program. That request may, or may not, necessitate a physical I/O. For example, on a read request the required record may already be in a memory buffer and therefore a physical I/O is not necessary.

marginal cost

> The cost of providing the service now, based upon the investment already made.

maturity level/milestone

> The degree to which BCM activities and processes have become standard business practice within an organisation.

metric

> Measurable element of a service process or function.

Operational Costs

> Those costs resulting from the day to day running of the IT Services section, e.g. staff costs, hardware maintenance and electricity, and relating to repeating payments whose effects can be measured within a short timeframe, usually less than the 12 month financial year.

Operational Level Agreement (OLA)

> An internal agreement covering the delivery of services which supports the IT organisation in their delivery of services.

Operations

> All activities and measures to enable and/or maintain the intended use of the ICT infrastructure.

opportunity cost (or true cost)

> The value of a benefit sacrificed in favour of an alternative course of action. That is the cost of using resources in a particular operation expressed in terms of foregoing the benefit that could be derived from the best alternative use of those resources.

organisational culture

> The whole of the ideas, corporate values, beliefs, practices, expectations about behaviour and daily customs that are shared by the employees in an organisation.

outsourcing

> The process by which functions performed by the organisation are contracted out for operation, on the organisation's behalf, by third parties.

overheads

> The total of indirect materials, wages and expenses.

Package Assembly/ Disassembly Device (PAD)

> A device that permits terminals which do not have an interface suitable for direct connection to a packet switched network to access such a network. A PAD converts data to/from packets and handles call set up and addressing.

page fault

> A program interruption that occurs when a page that is marked 'not in real memory' is referred to by an active page.

Paging

> The I/O necessary to read and write to and from the paging disks: real (not virtual) memory is needed to process data. With insufficient real memory, the operating system writes old pages to disk, and reads new pages from disk, so that the required data and instructions are in real memory.

PD0005

> Alternative title for the BSI publication A Code of Practice for IT Service Management.

percentage utilisation

> The amount of time that a hardware device is busy over a given period of time. For example, if the CPU is busy for 1800 seconds in a one hour period, its utilisation is said to be 50%.

Performance Criteria

> The expected levels of achievement, which are set within the SLA against specific Key Performance Indicators.

phantom line error

> A communications error reported by a computer system that is not detected by network monitoring equipment. It is often caused by changes to the circuits and network equipment (e.g. rerouting circuits at the physical level on a backbone network) while data communications is in progress.

physical I/O

> A read or write request from a program has necessitated a physical read or write operation on an I/O device.

prime cost

> The total cost of direct materials, direct labour and direct expenses. The term 'prime cost' is commonly restricted to direct production costs only and so does not customarily include direct costs of marketing or research and development.

PRINCE2

> The standard UK government method for Project Management.

priority

> Sequence in which an Incident or Problem needs to be resolved, based on impact and urgency.

Problem

> Unknown underlying cause of one or more Incidents.

Problem Management

> Process that minimises the effect on Customer(s) of defects in services and within the infrastructure, human errors and external events.

process

> A connected series of actions, activities, Changes etc, performed by agents with the intent of satisfying a purpose or achieving a goal.

Process Control

> The process of planning and regulating, with the objective of performing the process in an effective and efficient way.

programme

> A collection of activities and projects that collectively implement a new corporate requirement or function.

provider

> The organisation concerned with the provision of IT services.

Quality of Service

> An agreed or contracted level of service between a service Customer and a service provider.

queuing time

> Queuing time is incurred when the device, which a program wishes to use, is already busy. The program therefore has to wait in a queue to obtain service from that device.

RAID

> Redundant Array of Inexpensive Disks – a mechanism for providing data resilience for computer systems using mirrored arrays of magnetic disks.

> Different levels of RAID can be applied to provide for greater resilience.

reference data

> Information that supports the plans and action lists, such as names and addresses or inventories, which is indexed within the plan.

Release

> A collection of new and/or changed CIs, which are tested and introduced into the live environment together.

remote fixes

> Incidents or problems resolved without a member of the support staff visiting the physical location of the problems. Note: fixing incidents or problems remotely minimises the delay before the service is back to normal and are therefore usually cost effective.

Request For Change (RFC)

> Form, or screen, used to record details of a request for a change to any CI within an infrastructure or to procedures and items associated with the infrastructure.

resolution

> Action that will resolve an Incident. This may be a work around.

resource cost

> The amount of machine resource that a given task consumes. This resource is usually expressed in seconds for the CPU or the number of I/Os for a disk or tape device.

resource profile

> The total resource costs that are consumed by an individual on line transaction, batch job or program. It is usually expressed in terms of CPU seconds, number of I/Os and memory usage.

resource unit costs

> Resource units may be calculated on a standard cost basis to identify the expected (standard) cost for using a particular resource. Because computer resources come in many shapes and forms, units have to be established by logical groupings. Examples are:

a) CPU time or instructions

b) disk I/O

c) print line

d) communication transactions.

resources

The IT Services section needs to provide the Customers with the required services. The resources are typically computer and related equipment, software, facilities or organisational (people).

Return On Investment

The ratio of the cost of implementing a project, product or service and the savings as a result of completing the activity in terms of either internal savings, increased external revenue or a combination of the two. For instance, in simplistic terms, suppose the internal cost of ICT cabling of office moves is £100,000 per annum and a structured cabling system can be installed for £300,000. An ROI will be achieved after approximately three years.

return to normal phase

The phase within a business recovery plan which re establishes normal operations.

Risk

A measure of the exposure to which an organisation may be subjected. This is a combination of the likelihood of a business disruption occurring and the possible loss that may result from such business disruption.

Risk Analysis

The identification and assessment of the level (measure) of the risks calculated from the assessed values of assets and the assessed levels of threats to, and vulnerabilities of, those assets.

Risk Management

The identification, selection and adoption of countermeasures justified by the identified risks to assets in terms of their potential impact upon services if failure occurs, and the reduction of those risks to an acceptable level.

Risk reduction measure

Measures taken to reduce the likelihood or consequences of a business disruption occurring (as opposed to planning to recover after a disruption).

role

A set of responsibilities, activities and authorisations.

roll in, roll out (RIRO)

Used on some systems to describe swapping.

Rotational Position Sensing

A facility that is employed on most mainframes and some minicomputers. When a seek has been initiated, the system can free the path from a disk drive to a controller for use by another disk drive, while it is waiting for the required data to come under the read/write heads (latency). This facility usually improves the overall performance of the I/O subsystem.

second line support

Where the fault cannot be resolved by first line or requires time to be resolved or local attendance.

Security Management

The process of managing a defined level of security on information and services.

Security Manager

The Security Manager is the role that is responsible for the Security Management process in the service provider organisation. The person is responsible for fulfilling the security demands as specified in the SLA, either directly or through delegation by the Service Level Manager. The Security Officer and the Security Manager work closely together.

Security Officer

The Security Officer is responsible for assessing the business risks and setting the security policy. As such, this role is the counterpart of the Security Manager and resides in the Customer's business organisation. The Security Officer and the Security Manager work closely together.

seek time

Occurs when the disk read/write heads are not positioned on the required track. It describes the elapsed time taken to move heads to the right track.

segregation of duties

Separation of the management or execution of certain duties or of areas of responsibility is required in order to prevent and reduce opportunities for unauthorised modification or misuse of data or service.

self insurance

A decision to bear the losses that could result from a disruption to the business as opposed to taking insurance cover on the risk.

Service

One or more IT systems that enable a business process.

Service achievement

The actual service levels delivered by the IT organisation to a Customer within a defined lifespan.

Service Catalogue

Written statement of IT services, default levels and options.

Service Desk

The single point of contact within the IT organisation for Users of IT services.

Service Improvement Programme (SIP)

A formal project undertaken within an organisation to identify and introduce measurable improvements within a specified work area or work process.

Service Level

The expression of an aspect of a service in definitive and quantifiable terms.

Service Level Agreement (SLA)

Written agreement between a service provider and the Customer(s) that documents agreed service levels for a service.

Service Level Management (SLM)

The process of defining, agreeing, documenting and managing the levels of Customer IT service that are required and cost justified.

Service Management

Management of Services to meet the Customer's requirements.

Service provider

Organisation supplying services or products to Customers. This can be either internal to the organisation or external (third party).

Service quality plan

The written plan and specification of internal targets designed to guarantee the agreed service levels.

Service Request

Every Incident not being a failure in the IT Infrastructure.

Services

The deliverables of the IT Services organisation as perceived by the Customers; the services do not consist merely of making computer resources available for Customers to use.

severity code

Simple code assigned to problems and known errors, indicating the seriousness of their effect on the quality of service. It is the major means of assigning priority for resolution.

simulation modelling

Using a program to simulate computer processing by describing in detail the path of a job or transaction. It can give extremely accurate results. Unfortunately, it demands a great deal of time and effort from the modeller. It is most beneficial in extremely large or time critical systems where the margin for error is very small.

soft fault

The situation in a virtual memory system when the operating system has detected that a page of code or data was due to be reused, i.e. it is on a list of 'free' pages, but it is still actually in memory. It is now rescued and put back into service.

Software Configuration Item (SCI)

As 'Configuration Item', excluding hardware and services.

software environment

Software used to support the application such as operating system, database management system, development tools, compilers, and application software.

software library

A controlled collection of SCIs designated to keep those with like status and type together and segregated from unlike, to aid in development, operation and maintenance.

software work unit

>Software work is a generic term devised to represent a common base on which all calculations for workload usage and IT resource capacity are then based. A unit of software work for I/O type equipment equals the number of bytes transferred; and for central processors it is based on the product of power and CPU time.

solid state devices

>Memory devices that are made to appear as if they are disk devices. The advantages of such devices are that the service times are much faster than real disks since there is no seek time or latency. The main disadvantage is that they are much more expensive.

spec sheet

>Specifies in detail what the Customer wants (external) and what consequences this has for the service provider (internal) such as required resources and skills.

stakeholder

>Any individual or group who has an interest, or 'stake,' in the IT service organisation or a CSIP.

standard cost

>A predetermined calculation of how much costs should be under specified working conditions. It is built up from an assessment of the value of cost elements and correlates technical specifications and the quantification of materials, labour and other costs to the prices and/or wages expected to apply during the period in which the standard cost is intended to be used. Its main purposes are to provide bases for control through variance accounting, for the valuation of work in progress and for fixing selling prices.

standard costing

>A technique that uses standards for costs and revenues for the purposes of control through variance analysis.

stand by arrangements

>Arrangements to have available assets, which have been identified as replacements should primary assets be unavailable following a business disruption. Typically, these include accommodation, IT systems and networks, telecommunications and sometimes people.

storage occupancy

>A defined measurement unit that is used for storage type equipment to measure usage. The unit value equals the number of bytes stored.

Super User

>In some organisations it is common to use 'Expert' Users (commonly known as Super or Expert Users) to deal with first line support problems and queries. This is typically in specific application areas, or geographical locations, where there is not the requirement for full time support staff. This valuable resource however needs to be carefully coordinated and utilised.

surcharging

>Charging business Users a premium rate for using resources at peak times.

swapping

>The reaction of the operating system to insufficient real memory: swapping occurs when too many tasks are perceived to be competing for limited resources. It is the

physical movement of an entire task (e.g. all real memory pages of an address space may be moved at one time from main storage to auxiliary storage).

system

An integrated composite that consists of one or more of the processes, hardware, software, facilities and people, that provides a capability to satisfy a stated need or objective.

terminal emulation

Software running on an intelligent device, typically a PC or workstation, which allows that device to function as an interactive terminal connected to a host system. Examples of such emulation software includes IBM 3270 BSC or SNA, ICL C03, or Digital VT100.

terminal I/O

A read from, or a write to, an on line device such as a VDU or remote printer.

third line support

Where specialists skills (e.g. development/engineer) or contracted third party support is required.

third party supplier

An enterprise or group, external to the Customer's enterprise, which provides services and/or products to that Customer's enterprise.

thrashing

A condition in a virtual storage system where an excessive proportion of CPU time is spent moving data between main and auxiliary storage.

threat

An indication of an unwanted incident that could impinge on the system in some way. Threats may be deliberate (e.g. wilful damage) or accidental (e.g. operator error).

Total Cost of Ownership (TCO)

Calculated including depreciation, maintenance, staff costs, accommodation, and planned renewal.

tree structures

In data structures, a series of connected nodes without cycles. One node is termed the 'root' and is the starting point of all paths; other nodes termed 'leaves' terminate the paths.

unabsorbed overhead

Any Indirect Cost that cannot be apportioned to a specific Customer.

underpinning contract

A contract with an external supplier covering delivery of services that support the IT organisation in their delivery of services.

unit costs

Costs distributed over individual component usage. For example, it can be assumed that, if a box of paper with 1000 sheets costs £10, then each sheet costs 1p. Similarly if a CPU costs £1m a year and it is used to process 1,000 jobs that year, each job costs on average £1,000.

urgency

Measure of the business criticality of an Incident or Problem based on the impact and on the business needs of the Customer.

User

The person who uses the service on a day to day basis.

Utility Cost Centre (UCC)

A cost centre for the provision of support services to other cost centres.

variance analysis

A variance is the difference between planned, budgeted or standard cost and actual cost (or revenues). Variance analysis is an analysis of the factors that have caused the difference between the pre determined standards and the actual results. Variances can be developed specifically related to the operations carried out in addition to those mentioned above.

version

An identified instance of a Configuration Item within a product breakdown structure or configuration structure for the purpose of tracking and auditing change history. Also used for software Configuration Items to define a specific identification released in development for drafting, review or modification, test or production.

version identifier

A version number; version date; or version date and time stamp.

virtual memory system

A system that enhances the size of hard memory by adding an auxiliary storage layer residing on the hard disk.

Virtual Storage Interrupt (VSI)

An ICL VME term for a page fault.

vulnerability

A weakness of the system and its assets, which could be exploited by threats.

warm stand by

See 'intermediate recovery'.

waterline

The lowest level of detail relevant to the Customer.

Work-around

Method of avoiding an Incident or Problem, either from a temporary fix or from a technique that means the Customer is not reliant on a particular aspect of the service that is known to have a Problem.

workloads

In the context of Capacity Management Modelling, a set of forecasts that detail the estimated resource usage over an agreed planning horizon. Workloads generally represent discrete business applications and can be further sub divided into types of work (interactive, timesharing, batch).

WORM (Device)

Optical read only disks, standing for Write Once Read Many.

APPENDIX B PROCESS THEORY

B.1 Process theory

This Appendix provides a general introduction to process theory and practice, which is the basis for the ITIL process models. An awareness of 'process' comes through process models that define workflows and provide guidance on performing it. A process model enables understanding and helps to articulate the distinctive features of a process.

A process can be defined as:

> *a connected series of actions, activities, changes etc., performed by agents with the intent of satisfying a purpose or achieving a goal.*

Process Control can similarly be defined as:

> *the process of planning and regulating, with the objective of performing a process in an effective and efficient way.*

Processes, once defined, should be under control; once under control, they can be repeated and become manageable. Degrees of control over processes can be defined, and then metrics can be built in to manage the control process.

The output produced by a process has to conform to operational norms that are derived from business objectives. If products conform to the set norm, the process can be considered effective (because it can be repeated, measured and managed). If the activities are carried out with a minimum effort, the process can also be considered efficient.

Process results metrics should be incorporated in regular management reports.

B.1.1 The product oriented organisation

Process activities exist in many organisations. However, they are often carried out throughout an organisation, but without any process oriented coordination. This results in problems which have to be addressed during process implementation. Some examples include:

- processes lacking a clear purpose and focus on business results
- similar processes with inconsistent approaches
- actions or processes performed many times instead of once
- activities that are missing
- no focus on existing business oriented results.

B.1.2 Moving towards a process-oriented organisation

Since processes and their activities run through an organisation, they should be mapped and coordinated by process managers. Figure B.1 shows how process activities may be assigned to people in several different organisational units. The simple box diagram indicates the apparent consecutive flow of processes in a linear sequence. Reality is better reflected in the organisational view, where the flow is clearly non linear and where it is possible to think of delays and interactions that might take place.

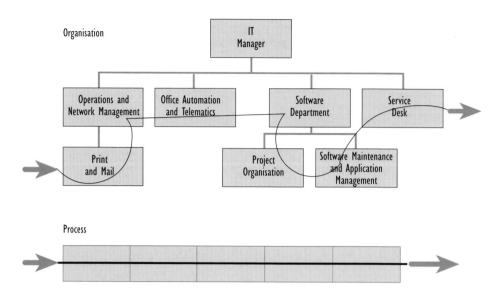

Figure B.1 – Process mapped to organisational unit

In a product oriented organisation, the flow of activities and processes in Figure B.1 is not generally recognised at all; the focus is on the product, and management and control is often lacking. The evidence is in the lack of any useful metrics related to the production process, because the process activities are not clear or even not identified.

B.1.3   The process approach

The model shown in Figure B.2 is a generic process model. Data enters the process, is processed, data comes out, the outcome is measured and reviewed. This very basic description underpins any process description. A process is always organised around a goal. The main output of that process is the result of that goal.

Working with defined processes is a novelty for many organisations. By defining what the organisation's activities are, which inputs are necessary and which outputs will result from the process, it is possible to work in a more efficient and effective manner. Measuring and steering the activities increases this efficacy. Finally, by adding norms to the process, it is possible to add quality measures to the output.

The approach underpins the 'Plan, Do, Check, Act' cycle of any Quality Management System. Plan the purpose of the process in such a way that the process action can be audited for successful achievement and, if necessary, improved.

The output produced by a process has to conform to operational norms that are derived from business objectives. If the products conform to the set norm, the process can be considered effective. If the activities are also carried out with a minimum effort, the process can also be considered efficient. Process measurement results should be incorporated in regular management reports.

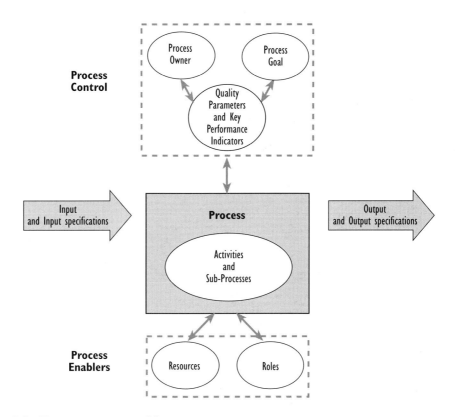

Figure B.2 – The generic process model

'Norms' define certain conditions that the results should meet. Defining norms introduces quality aspects to the process. Even before starting, it is important to think about what the outcome should look like. This enables:

- inputs and activities to be considered beforehand because what to do is known

- effective measurement because what to measure is known

- assessment of whether the result fulfilled expectations because what to expect is known.

Defining objective norms is a tedious task and also often very complex since objectivity can often be subjective (to slightly misquote Woody Allen).

To discover whether or not activities are contributing optimally to the business goal of the process, measure their effectiveness on a regular basis. Measuring allows comparison between what has actually been done to what the organisation set out to do and to consider the improvement that may be needed.

APPENDIX C FRAMEWORK FOR EVALUATION OF ORGANISATIONS

The maturity of an IT organisation can be defined as a stage within the Growth Model shown in Figure C.1.

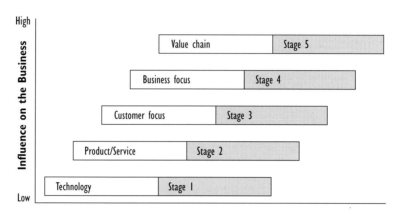

Figure C.1 – IT Organisation Growth Model

Table C.1 describes some of the key characteristics for each stage in the Organisation Growth model, and can be used to determine which stage describes the IT organisation. It can also be used to define future requirements for role characteristics.

Stage	Element	Characteristics
Technology	Vision and strategy	Business views role of IT as Infrastructure provider (hardware, software and network provider). No clear vision statement on role of IT.
	Steering	Principally driven by cost. Stability, availability and performance of IT platforms and networks are the main focus and implicit steering parameters.
	Processes	Focus on Systems and Network Management, IT design and implementation.
	People	Technology excellence.
	Technology	Systems and Network Management tools are independently purchased and used to manage technology subsets.
	Culture	'We are IT experts'. There is little interaction or understanding of providing 'services' to the business.

Stage	Element	Characteristics
Product/ Service	Vision and strategy	The IT organisation recognises that it delivers a portfolio of products and services to the business. Evidence of IT strategic planning, little input from business.
	Steering	Services are defined in technology terms such as bandwidth, processing performance, disc capacity. Reporting and steering on IT defined parameters.
	Processes	Strong focus on ITIL Service Support processes and the more operational aspects of the ITIL Service Delivery processes, such as performance measurement and tuning, availability measurement and building resilience. Reporting mechanisms are used to improve product and service performance.
	People	Clearer definition of IT functions. Recognition of first and second line expertise.
	Technology	More product standardisation. Design of architectures and integration into management tools and systems.
	Culture	Team and product orientation. Customer awareness and promotion towards Customers.
Customer Focus	Vision and strategy	IT seen as IT service provider. IT strategy linked to business strategy.
	Steering	Service Level Agreements steer IT. Change Management integrated into project structure for ensuring smooth handover from new IT development.
	Processes	Service Level Management, formalised Account Management. More focus on planning aspects in delivery processes.
		Support processes deliver clear service and Customer related performance. Process reporting underpins service level agreements.
	People	Service Management training and defined activities and roles. Evidence of process ownership, Formalised Account Management and Service Management roles in place.
	Technology	Integrated systems and Service Management platforms, manageability built into technology designs and solutions. Operational requirements defined for handover into production environment.
	Culture	Customer satisfaction.

Business Focus	Vision and strategy	IT is seen as a partner to the business. IT demonstrates strategy realisation for the business. IT strategy input to business strategy making process.
	Steering	IT strategic goals, IT proposals made and discussed at board level. Business priority and risk assessments of investing and not investing in IT. Service levels are defined more in business terms, such as 'business transactions processed', 'availability of business functionality'.
	Processes	Business and IT alignment processes. Strong Integration between Systems development and IT Service Management processes.
		Processes deliver 'dashboard steering information'. Service delivery and support processes integrated. Delivery processes deliver sound planning and advice to the business.
	People	Business intelligence and business competencies. CIO role and CTO role. Equal roles in business and IT.
	Technology	R and D and technology pilots. An enterprise wide management framework exists defining integrated service and systems management toolsets.
	Culture	The IT Organisation provides help and advice to the business.
Value chain	Vision and strategy	IT is seen as business enabler. IT helps shape and drive business Change and is seen as a value added partner that helps determine business strategy.
	Steering	IT is steered on added value to the business. Business improvements through use of IT.
	Processes	Business and IT strategy making. The IT organisation ensures seamless integration with systems development and all other IT suppliers in the value chain to manage real end to end services for the business.
	People	Strategy making, business planning, managing partners and suppliers. Infrastructure Integrators.
	Technology	Technology interaction between suppliers. Solutions integration.
	Culture	The IT Organisation enables the business.

Table C.1 – IT growth model characteristics

APPENDIX D A SERVICE MANAGEMENT CASE STUDY

A **company** consisting of some 3,500 staff with an IT section 300 strong, decided five years ago to start examining the options for the implementation of Service Management within their IT department. The IT staff were split, with around 130 working in operations and support, and approximately 170 working in development, supporting the many in house developed systems. In 1996 their IT infrastructure principally consisted of a number of centralised mainframes, with many client PCs distributed throughout the Headquarters and Regional Offices. A member of their senior management team attended an IT Service Management training course and it was decided to instigate an external, benchmarking audit to establish a starting reference point. Also around this time the existing Help Desk system was replaced.

The external audit identified many initial problem areas with only four processes, Service Level Management, Contingency Planning, Help Desk and Software Control and Distribution having any real elements of control. Some of the processes particularly Configuration Management and Cost Management were particularly immature. The major issues identified with the Service Management processes were:

- a lack of involvement of development staff in the operability aspects of services and software
- a 'task oriented' culture relying on people's knowledge rather than documented procedures
- processes dispersed among functions rather than focused
- procedures with limited scope, with some areas of IT being independent of the procedures
- a lack of communication between isolated processes
- an IT Disaster Recovery plan limited in scope and effectiveness.

Based on the outcome of this audit, the IT Manager produced the objectives for the following company year and they included an IT objective stating:

> **All Service Management processes (excluding Cost Management) will achieve 'control' level by the end of the company year, April 1998.**

The 'control level' above is the same as the **control level** illustrated within the Service management Process Maturity Framework (SPMF). A concerted programme of improvement was instigated in all nine of the selected Service Management processes, especially within the immature processes. An overall Project Manager was appointed to control and coordinate the overall CSIP and a second set of independent, external consultants were contracted to assist the **company** with the design and implementation of the process improvements. The first action that taken was to assign a process owner for each of the nine processes being tackled. Some of the process owners were full time and others were involved on a part time basis. Each process owner was responsible for identifying a process team and coordinating the working of the team. The process team members were drawn from all of the operational and support areas of IT and all of the process team members worked on a part time basis on Service Management activities. This ensured that the processes developed were acceptable to all IT operational units. Early within the project, the external consultants facilitated training workshops on each of the processes involved, with the individual process teams. Standard document templates were agreed and actions put it place to ensure that each process produced a standard set of documentation:

- a process framework document
- a process improvement plan
- a set of formal process targets.

While the process teams were developing the process improvements and documentation, a set of one day Service Management overview courses were developed and run for all IT staff. The importance of Service Management and the quality of Customer service were emphasised and endorsed through all levels of IT management.

At this stage some of the process owners had obtained the Service Management Foundation certificate and others hadn't, so it was decided that all process owners should complete the Foundation course and examination and this was done. Two or three other, additional key members of staff also acquired the full Service Management Manager's certificate. Additionally two seminars where also held for all IT staff on the importance of Customer service in the delivery of IT services.

The process documentation was completed and reviewed by all of the process owners and then distributed for a wider QA throughout all areas of IT. In parallel with this activity the detailed process and procedural documentation was also developed, based wherever possible on the existing processes and procedures. All of these activities were tasks with associated milestones on the individual process, project plans. The actual process improvement activities and responsibilities were also tasks and milestones contained within the same plan. These plans were reviewed initially on a monthly basis and then weekly as the project neared completion. During the progress of these plans the Remedy tool was extended to also provide Change Management, Configuration Management and Problem Management functionality, underpinning the enhanced processes. An interim mini assessment was completed during the project some three to four months before the completion date, to identify areas of weakness or shortfall. The areas identified were fed back to each of the process owners and where necessary, remedial actions were developed and incorporated into their process improvement projects.

The second full external audit was commenced at the end of the **company** year (April 1998) and the results were that seven of the processes reached '**integrated**' status and the remaining two reached well into the '**control**' level, of the SPMF. The project was signed off as a complete success having exceeded its primary objective, the delivery of nine '**control**' status Service Management processes.

Flushed with the success of the Service Management project, the management commitment to the processes waned. Some of process owners moved on, others returned to their primary roles and not all of them were replaced. Some of the processes retained their process owners and were sufficiently mature to continue with their improvement plans. Others lost their focus, were less mature and stagnated. In one or two cases they even started to decay.

Over the next two years, against this backdrop, the IT organisation was now facing different drivers for more distributed technology, upgraded PC Desktop and Laptop hardware, software and associated PC file servers, upgraded LAN and WAN systems and the replacement of the ICL mainframe with mid range solutions. There was also a significant business demand for the development of the web servers into a major 'n tier', global Internet site. This was concurrent with several major software developments and software releases throughout this period of change. There was also the spectre of the Y2K situation looming on the horizon.

Once the hurdle of Y2K was overcome and all of the major infrastructure enhancements had been completed the focus again turned to Service Management. The objectives for the **company** year 2000/2001 were again set by the IT Manager, and this time:

> **All ten Service Management processes will achieve 'integrated' level by the end of the company year, April 2001.**

The benchmarking audit report from April 1998 was reviewed and the major recommendations revisited:

- priority should be given to address those processes below **'integration'** level
- Operational Level Agreements (OLAs) should be further developed, measured and reviewed
- Business Continuity Plans should be fully developed to incorporate the PC and LAN arena
- methods for identifying total actual Customer costs and breakdown of those costs should be implemented
- supplier relationships and contracts should be reviewed, enhanced and instigated to ensure consistency with SLAs
- as the CMDB is more fully populated advantage should be taken to integrate it more fully with all other Service Management and Operational Management processes and tools.

The pressure was back on the Service Management process owners. Rapidly, replacement process owners were appointed for those processes that were ownerless. The one process that had increased significantly in its maturity and its effectiveness during the previous two years was of course Contingency Planning. The Y2K effect had raised the profile of what had now evolved into business Continuity Planning and with Director level sponsorship was not only covering IT services, but also had been enhanced to cover business process and workplace recovery plans.

An overall Programme Manager was appointed and the project team of process owners was reconvened. This time representatives from the development area were also included within the overall project and the project team. It was agreed early within the project that the 'development lifecycle' would be reviewed and the essential Service Management processes included at the appropriate points within the revised version. This was to be documented, agreed and implemented, so that early within the design and development of new systems consideration and account would be given to the Service Management processes and procedures. The commitment, buy in and approval of senior IT management were obtained and the project was initiated. Again, a crucial aspect of the running of the project was the regular project review meeting involving all of the process owners and the development representatives.

One of the early tasks of each of the process owners was to review and revise all of the process documents developed in the earlier Service Management project. This principally focused on:

- reviewing and improving the process framework document, especially in the areas of interfaces and dependencies on other Service Management processes, particularly Financial Management which hadn't really been addressed previously
- developing and implementing a revised process improvement plan for each process

- reviewing the use and effectiveness of the formal process reports, targets and metrics, with considerable enhancement in all areas and all processes.

Each process owner reviewed the documentation of all of the other processes, to ensure that all of their dependencies were included. Once these had been approved within the project team they were all submitted to a wider QA review throughout IT.

The training of IT staff was reviewed and it was decided that all IT staff would be expected to complete the Service Management course and examination. Rather than send staff to external courses a **company** tailored version of the Foundation course was developed and delivered internally with all of the process owners being involved in the delivery of the sessions and assignments, on their own processes. The course has been an outstanding success not only explaining the theory but also the process practices within the **company**. Subsequent to this a tailored version of the Network Services Management course was also developed with equal success. Both courses have been delivered a number of times.

The use of tools in underpinning the processes was also reviewed. The automated use of Operational Management tools was developed, and automated alarm and incident interfaces engineered into the Help Desk system. The system was further developed and enhanced in all of the existing process areas, with some additional aspects of Service Level Management and Availability Management also being incorporated. Financial Management was also rapidly being developed, with considerable assistance from other process owners and the **company** Finance Department.

Again the frequency of the project review meetings increased as the prospect of an external benchmark audit loomed. Again a mini audit was taken to identify the major risk areas and a number of areas were identified. Remedial actions were incorporated into plans and subsequently implemented. Prior to the full external audit, process owners were each given another process to review and assess for maturity in preparation for the full audit.

The full external benchmark audit was completed in April 2001 and although only five of the processes achieved '**integrated status**' the remainder retained their '**control status**'. The external auditing organisation commented that it was the highest Service Management assessment that they had seen, even though the overall **company** objective was not achieved, they were impressed by the quality and effectiveness that they had observed.

It just goes to show that the process of continuous improvement is an ongoing one and the process goes on ...

APPENDIX E PRAGMATIC APPROACHES TO SERVICE MANAGEMENT IMPLEMENTATION

E.1 Types of approach

There is no universal 'right way' of implementing Service Management within an organisation. However there are a number of different approaches that have been used by organisations in the past to achieve significant degrees of success. These different approaches can be categorised in to three major types:

1 Single process approach

2 Multi process approach

3 All processes approach.

Each organisation needs to evaluate the alternative approaches and select the most appropriate for them in their current situation. The approach adopted by an organisation will depend upon a number of factors:

- the senior management commitment
- the allocated budget
- resource availability
- the skills and knowledge within the organisation
- the culture and organisational structure
- the business and IT vision and strategy
- the tools and technology
- the demands for 'business as usual'.

The approach selected for implementation by an organisation should be reviewed at regular intervals to ensure that it is still appropriate. As organisations and their Service Management processes develop the appropriateness of the approach selected will Change and it is more likely that a 'multi' or 'all' process approach will be required. Therefore stage reviews should be scheduled to assess the appropriateness of the approach selected and to adapt the implementation plans if the approach needs to Change.

It is important to recognise and achieve 'quick wins' during the implementation of any CSIP or process improvement. However, it is vitally important that long term objectives are not jeopardised for the sake of achieving these 'quick wins'.

An organisation where the maturity of the Service Management processes is at the lower levels of the SPMF can use any of the different approaches. However the further an organisation progresses up the maturity levels the more the 'multi process' or 'all processes' approaches have to be adopted. To reach level four and above the only approach that can be adopted is the 'all processes' technique. The details of each of the individual approaches within the three types listed above are covered in the next three sections.

E.2   Single process approaches

This involves the implementation, development or improvement of a single process at a particular moment in time. These approaches are normally, only used in the short term because it quickly becomes evident that significant improvements cannot be made by instigating enhancements within a single process. Therefore organisations rapidly move to either a 'multi' or 'all' process approach. These approaches are normally triggered by internal IT initiatives. Examples of the single process approach are discussed in this Section.

E.2.1   Problem Management approach

This involves implementing a basic Problem Management process and identifying those areas that are causing the most 'pain and disruption' to the organisation. This can be calculated as either:

■ the most pain and disruption to the internal IT processes and resources used within IT

■ the IT perceived view of the most pain and disruption caused by IT processes on the business and its processes.

Once either of these activities have been completed then the next areas causing the greatest 'pain and disruption', either to the business or IT, can be targeted for improvement.

E.2.2   Service Desk and Incident Management approach

Implementing Incident and Problem Management are obvious starting points. Having a Service Desk that is a true central point of contact and able to follow exacting processes with KPIs that are monitored and managed can show dramatic service improvements when first implemented.

This can be a valuable weapon for gaining support from sponsors and improving relationships with the Customers. Customers always respond well to a warm, friendly, courteous and helpful support analyst at the first point of call. First impressions are massively important in this respect.

Significant gains can be won in a rapid and cost effective way by adopting a Customer Service Culture and focusing on achieving simple KPIs such as improvements to the speed of call answering and ensuring availability of the Service Desk. The Incident Management process can then be used to develop trends in the numbers, types and impacts of Incidents. This information can then be used to indicate the order in which areas of improvement should be tackled, in a similar manner to the previous approach.

E.2.3   Change Management approach

This approach is preferred in some organisations that find themselves in the 'vicious circle' of:

Failing Changes, causing incidents, leading to problems necessitating more Changes etc.

Implementing a single centralised Change Management process can be used to break this circle and bring some quick control to the situation.

Many organisations see Change Management as an important focus in providing stability during a Service Management implementation. Bringing visibility and impact analysis to all IT Changes can have dramatic effects on service availability and Customer service. Some organisations have had significant quick wins by implementing Change Management on a specific service initially and using this as the start point for both a Service Management implementation and longer term Change Management initiatives.

Movements, Additions and Changes

Many organisations suffer from poor service delivery to recently appointed employees. This process is often very complicated and involves many differing aspects of service provision. Typically, to prepare for a new employee, furniture and IT equipment need to be procured. IT equipment needs to be configured and delivered at the correct time. Floor points may need to be made live and patch panels connected. Access to networks need to be authorised and many other aspects of a new starter process may need to be invoked.

This can be complicated by the business requiring entry into this process at different stages. During the deployment of Change Management it may be beneficial to separate out the new starter process or Movements, Additions and Changes (MACs) element and run this as a separate entity managed through the Change Management function. Significant service improvements have been gained by organisations adopting the implementation of a new starter process as a first step.

E.2.4   Implementation by stealth

This, unfortunately very popular, approach to implementation is included in this Section as a cautionary tale. It is to be avoided at all costs.

Do not do this

This approach of implementing the process, without the visibility of a distinct cost-centre or project code, is by stealth (undercover). It consists of attempting to implement/adjust existing processes (to be conformant to best practice) as an adjunct to new IT projects. The solution is at best piecemeal. This approach is highly problematic, as there can be no timeframe, no established reporting/measurement structure, processes change spasmodically and, by definition, there is no real management buy-in. This approach leads to frustration and will lose commitment from all participants and stakeholders.

E.3   Multi process approaches

These involve the implementation, development or improvement of a number of processes concurrently. These approaches are often either initiated by, or involve, considerable discussion with the business and/or the IT Customers. Examples of this approach are provided in this Section.

E.3.1   The Continuous Service Improvement Programme (CSIP)

The philosophy of adopting a CSIP and changing the working culture to think in this way is an important part of striving for improvements within an organisation. The CSIP should focus on all aspects of service provision. The objectives of the CSIP can include a variety of other initiatives aimed at improving service, cultures or perhaps gaining a competitive edge.

The approach consists of the development and maintenance of an overall CSIP. This would be used to contain details of all of the activities identified as contributing to the improvement of IT service delivery. This can then be used to coordinate, plan and schedule the improvement activities, in priority order of impact on service quality, subject to resource and budget availability.

E.3.2   Customer Satisfaction Surveys (CSS)/Business Impact approach

This approach consists of one of the following:

■ conducting a CSS in order to determine the Customer perception of the current quality of IT service delivery. A CSS will assist with understanding how far the organisation has improved when discussions take place on the progress of the project. The analysis and subsequent results of the survey can be used to target those process areas that will return the most benefit to the major Customers of IT

■ implementing the initial elements of an IT Service Continuity process and completing an initial Business Impact Analysis (BIA). The purpose of this is not only to determine business impact and recovery but also to determine those areas and processes that are currently causing the greatest disruption to the business during normal operation.

The results from either the Customer Survey or the BIA can then be used to target those processes and areas that are going to yield the greatest benefit to the business and the Customers of IT.

Most organisations or companies have business critical systems or areas where Customers or Users would like to see improvements in their service provision. An in depth look at this would result in a clear understanding of what extent of disruption is being experienced by the business in these key areas. This would provide valuable feedback as to where to start the implementation. A BIA is one of the most valuable deliverables from the Service Management processes.

E.3.3   SWOT Analysis approach

This approach would consist of completing a Strengths, Weaknesses, Opportunities and Threats (SWOT) analysis. This could then be used to:

■ internally:
  - build, develop and improve the Strengths within IT organisation (e.g. the Service Desk and Incident Management)
  - remove and reduce the areas of Weakness (e.g. poor service availability)
■ externally:
  - grasp and realise the Opportunities (e.g. work with specialist and strategic partners)
  - reduce and counter any Threats (e.g. take over or outsource).

E.3.4   Benchmark approach

Benchmarking will establish the extent of existing compliance to 'best practice' and will help in understanding the scope required by the CSIP to achieve terms of reference. Deciding what the Key Performance Indicators (KPIs) are going to be and then measuring against them will give solid management information for future improvement and targets.

A benchmark exercise would be used as the first stage in this approach. This could be either one or other of:

- **an internal benchmark:** completed internally using resources from within the organisation to assess the maturity of the Service Management processes against a reference framework. The framework used could be the SPMF, the BSI or the OGC variants. The BSI and OGC provide a set of questions that can be used for self assessment
- **an external benchmark:** this would be completed by an external third party company. Most of these have their own proprietary model for the assessment of Service Management process maturity.

The results and recommendations contained within the benchmarking review can then be used to identify and rectify areas of weakness within the IT Service Management processes.

E.3.5   Service Target approach

Often Service Management practitioners look at service levels first. It is commonplace for support staff to complain of Customers' high expectations and therefore feel establishing Customer requirements should be the first place to start.

Understanding the minimum levels of service that the Customers require to achieve their own objectives can often be a challenging but worthwhile place to commence the implementation. This can often provide enlightenment for end Users as well as support teams. However it is worth noting that unless Customer expectation can be aligned with the cost to the Customer it can also be difficult to gain agreement on service levels.

This approach would consist of developing simple or 'pilot' service targets in terms of:

- service Availability
- User service response time
- Change target schedules
- service Incident resolution times
- responses received from CSSs.

These service targets can then be used to drive forward the most appropriate Service Management processes required to support the achievement of these provisional service targets. The provisional targets can then form the basis of the agreed SLAs once IT is confident the processes can support the agreed SLA targets.

E.4   All processes approaches

This involves the implementation, development or improvement of all ten Service Management processes simultaneously. There is only one approach.

E.4.1   All processes simultaneously

This approach of developing and improving all processes simultaneously can be driven in a number of ways:

- business/IT strategy and vision
- CSIP
- benchmark.

Organisations have achieved this most effectively by taking *small* steps in all of the processes concurrently. This needs to be coordinated by a single owner managing one overall Service Management CSIP. Individual process owners should then have an individual CSIP for their process. This is the only approach that will work once processes start to reach the higher levels (four and five) of the SPMF, because of the interdependence between processes. Regular team meetings must be held between the ten process owners and the CSIP coordinator in order to ensure smooth progression of all of the CSIPs.

E.5   Additional considerations

E.5.1   Introduction

This Section is intended as a supplement to the previous and comprehensive Sections of this publication where more exacting and detailed explanations exist on how to implement Service Management. The considerations are based on practical experiences of implementing IT Service Management and have been collected from a variety of first hand experiences.

It seeks to offer practical advice for IT or Programme Managers to consider when building their plans and beginning the process of implementing Service Management.

Some factors for consideration

Programme Managers should consider a number of factors as discussed in Section E.1, before deciding on where, when or how within the organisation to commence the initial Service Management implementation. Giving some thought to these factors and other points made in this Section will help underpin the future momentum of the initiative.

Additional factors and considerations are listed at the end of this Section in Table E.1.

The chicken or the egg?

When implementing Service Management some of the initial discussions or questions centre on how best to begin the implementation phase of the CSIP. If the all processes approach were not practical, what would be the definitive or most suitable ITIL discipline to adopt in the first instance and are there any disciplines that should be avoided during the early stages of Service Management Implementation? Is it better to commence with the process design, roll out integrated Service Management toolsets or begin the training of individuals in the required skills and background knowledge? The following points will consider some of the more common approaches to Service Management implementation. Additionally included are some suggestions that would not perhaps be considered as a natural place to start the CSIP.

E.5.2   Quick wins and foundations

ITIL methodology advises that when implementing any project to it is advisable to secure appropriate senior sponsorship. Often it may be necessary to demonstrate progress to a sponsor. Being able to achieve a quick return on this investment will help the business case to secure a greater commitment or budgetary approval.

All projects of this type will be expensive and finding ways of gaining support for the initiatives will serve to provide important momentum to the project and may secure additional buy in from unsuspected quarters.

It is likely, as a result of the Business Impact Analysis, that there will be some clear indicators of where in the business quick wins are likely to be gained. Care should be taken not to compromise the longer term objectives of the CSIP but to lay some foundations that can be capitalised on later as the appropriate disciplines are deployed.

Deploying some elements of a particular discipline can achieve a short term reduction in resource drain or workload. If the organisation is experiencing significant problems, which have been attributed to obvious capacity issues, why not commence the implementation with a quick win here?

More important than which discipline to start with, would be achieving some firm foundations and processes that the CSIP can work with or from. Having laid some groundwork tactically it is possible to return to this discipline at a later stage with a more strategic approach.

E.5.3   Alternative approach

There is no guaranteed or recommended approach for achieving success when implementing Service Management. Each company considering a project of this type will have different considerations and criteria and may well have commercial pressures or other directives that have been the catalyst for the project to commence.

Many companies use widely differing technology, infrastructure and operating systems. Additionally companies can have a variety of support structures and levels of support expertise, all of which may have important and individual operational needs.

Specialist support teams may even operate successfully outside of common ITIL compliant practices or use a combination of existing process that work. It is commonplace for smaller companies not to have a Capacity Plan, for example, but to purchase additional capacity on demand. Larger companies such as Web Hosting or Internet Service Providers would need to adopt a more efficient Capacity Management policy to ensure availability of their managed environments and underpin their Customer's financial and strategic objectives.

Subsequently CSIPs often have differing catalysts and deploy Service Management disciplines particularly initially, in a variety of ways, all of which have experienced success.

E.5.4 Small steps, awareness campaigns, and hearts and minds

It will be critical to win the confidence of IT staff to ensure that they follow the new processes and adopt the best practice methodology and service culture necessary for success in a programme of service improvement.

Deliberate steps should be taken, therefore, to win the hearts and minds of all staff impacted by or involved in the project. Every opportunity should be sought to evangelise positively about the benefits of effective and efficient Service Management processes.

Thinking big in terms of strategy and planning but implementing in small steps has most often had great success. This has the benefit of less impact on existing working practices.

Too much information or process change at a busy time can be counterproductive, particularly if the support staff do not understand fully why this is being done. So small steps can allow time for support staff and personnel to become familiar with Service Management concepts. It can also allow staff time to engage in some ITIL training or awareness while they have time for peer pressure to work and for teams to interact with new Service Management process and functions.

E.5.5 Flexible approach

The ability to be flexible in all aspects of implementation will have many positive returns for the successful outcome of the implementation. Flexibility should be designed in wherever possible.

For example, the project staff would benefit from having appropriate qualifications and multiple skill sets. When recruitment is taking place for permanent roles or project staff, consider other relevant experiences and skill sets in Service Management disciplines as well as relevant skills and experience for the specific roles.

E.5.6 Service Management awareness

Team leaders and support analysts who fundamentally understand the relationship between other ITIL disciplines such as Availability, IT Service Continuity, Incident or Problem Management can go a long way to creating momentum for the project. This will assist in avoiding the obvious conflicts that can occur in these and other areas where close operational links would be required.

Additionally Project members also benefit from a depth of experience or knowledge around Service Management. Project initiators can work with other members of the project more effectively if they better understand the disciplines that are being implemented in parallel.

Commonality of language

An element often overlooked by Service Management practitioners is the confusion caused when using the language of Service Management. Incidents, Problems, Availability, Capacity etc. can mean many different things to support staff and Customers. Distribution of glossaries or standards can help avoid some of this confusion. This can be particularly useful during the early stages of a Service Management implementation.

Team building

Working during a period of considerable operational Change can have a very disruptive influence on many people who are uncomfortable with these Changes. This can prove very stressful and demanding and can drain resources and energy when trying to overcome objections coming from the resistance that will occur.

Dialogue can be particularly effective between all teams and departments when a strong team or corporate spirit exists. So considerations should be given to ways of building a strong team spirit and maintaining morale in the team.

Internal support team involvement

As a Service Management discipline is implemented support teams should be consulted whenever possible and especially prior to documentation or processes being designed. This gives the teams the opportunity to add value or suggest how they might prefer the interface to take place.

A good example of this would be Support Team Leaders being asked by Problem Management to discuss with the Change Manager a recently highlighted process shortfall, perhaps following an unauthorised but necessary Change out of working hours. The discussion might be around how best to deal with Emergency Changes that need to be retrospectively recorded.

E.5.7   Phased approach vs. 'Big Bang'

Adopting a staged approach to implementation may be sensible where there is a need to reduce the initial process re engineering or cost. It may be that securing financial commitments or budget approval from senior management would favour picking one discipline and implementing this first. Often even the simplest of Service Desk software can have a huge amount of functionality that is not being utilised.

Exploiting existing resources and toolsets and aligning them to ITIL practices can be cost effective and rapidly achieve solutions.

A 'Big Bang' approach will require a significant amount of preparation and underpinning process work. Any process re-engineering will need to be mature and fully documented, coupled with a level of understanding throughout the support operation of what the new process will be, where to find it, what value this will bring and, where necessary, what the penalties for non-compliance will be.

E.5.8   Pilot phase

One way of using the 'all-processes' approach while reducing the workload is to run a pilot phase implementation within the company across all the disciplines but deploying within a specific department. Companies deploying a range of disciplines in one swoop, but doing so within more IT-friendly departments, have experienced some considerable success.

This has the advantage of receiving all the benefits of running a Pilot project, such as being able to iron out teething troubles early on at a time of less pressure or visibility. It allows the team to test how well the disciplines are able to interface with each other. This will result in a smoother implementation within other departments that the business might consider more critical or challenging.

E.5.9   Considering future interface requirements

There are ten processes within Service Management, all of which have important interfaces to other elements of ITIL Methodology. Maximum efficiency can only be achieved once these interfaces are fully operational, providing essential information and links to all other disciplines.

When deploying Service Management disciplines, ensure that the documentation, process and tools have catered for all the interfaces that will be required in the future, even if they will not be required at the initial implementation.

This will save valuable process re engineering and documentation Changes later in the project.

E.5.10   Project timescales

The start date for each phase of the project should be carefully considered. The time of the year or the position within the business cycle coinciding with the start of each phase of the project or implementation can have a significant impact on the initial impetus and progress. Ensuring adequate and appropriate resource availability for an important phase of the project can prevent a slow down in momentum or prevent unwanted delays during the implementation cycle.

The skill and personality of the Project Manager selected to manage the introduction of the Service Management processes is also vital to the success of the project. Someone should be chosen who is well respected throughout the organisation, is senior, an experienced Project Manager, a good communicator and has a proven track record of successful project delivery.

E.5.11   Communication channels

A key requirement for successful implementation of any of the Service Management processes will be to open up channels of communication into the areas of the business that will be impacted by any service outages.

Equally the support teams required to do the analysis of this issue will need to feel they are having their workloads properly prioritised and that Service Management disciplines can support them in return.

Service Management staff will need to commence dialogues with business departments, Customers and the User community, impacted by the outages, to accept ownership and gain Users' support and information on the issues. The support teams looking into the issues will need to assist the Problem Management function when involved in such things as arbitration.

When deploying Problem or Change Management, for example, the support teams will need to feel that these functions will add value. Communication, particularly during times of Major Incident handling or Urgent Changes, can be frustrated by a lack of understanding of each other's roles and responsibilities. Good inter team dialogue will always expedite and underpin effective resolution.

E.5.12   Awareness campaign

Many companies have failed to capitalise on their awareness campaign ability to underpin the service improvement plan. There are a multitude of ways that the business can enlist support for the project by informing them of the current state of the project, what is coming next, why, and so on. Use of Internet and Intranet technology, e mail newsletters, publications, roadshows, etc.

can have a dramatic effect on the ability of the business to be made aware of the importance of the programme.

Steering groups

Consideration should be given to forming steering groups, which comprise a selection of business managers to act as departmental authorities. This provides a forum where IT can liaise with its Customers on matters of policy. For example, this forum should be sought for discussing Service Level Requirements or deciding security or corporate policy. Typically companies have had good success with overall ICT Steering Groups (ISG) and Desktop Steering Groups or similar committees.

Other key considerations

Consideration	Detail	Benefits
Review existing company infrastructure	Investigate the extent of issues. Are there bad processes, under resourced teams, poor infrastructure?	If the organisation has several key operational IT locations it may be beneficial to deploy distributed Problem Management, for example. This can have many positive aspects during major incident handling.
Current project plans	Evaluate what plans are currently scheduled or in the pipeline.	Conflicting projects can drain valuable resources and slow time critical stages of the implementation.
Known difficulties of implementation	Read ITIL manuals for known issues and problems that are likely to occur.	This will allow formulation strategies on how to overcome these difficulties ahead of them happening.
Establish momentum	Enlist support from other team leaders and respected managers and other influential people.	Using peer pressure can be very effective in establishing momentum for the project.
Existing tools, processes and skills	Establish full extent of existing documented processes and toolsets.	Existing toolsets can often have a surprising level of unused functionality, which can reduce costs and result in a quicker deployment.
Use of external skills and resources	Inclusion of external consultancy companies and resources within the Service Management project team.	Faster implementation of the processes with avoidance of pitfalls and possible problems.
Corporate culture	Influence the corporate culture to be service orientated. Encourage ownership and being Customer focused.	Investing in and adopting some of the softer Customer-focused skills will pay great dividends with the Customers. This can be an inexpensive way to improve service.

Other Key Considerations - continued

Consideration	Detail	Benefits
Training	Take available opportunities to promote and educate IT staff with best practice.	Securing buy in from other IT Staff is essential to maintain momentum during the project.
itSMF	Join the itSMF and attend regional forums to meet other IT professionals facing similar problems.	Networking with colleagues in similar positions can help with understanding similar issues. Attending forums and listening to case studies and practical suggestions can reap huge rewards.

Table E.1 – Other key considerations

APPENDIX F PRO-FORMAS

F.1 Process specification

When designing a new or revised process for any of the Service Management processes it is recommended that a Process Specification also be produced. The specification should be kept at a fairly high level but it needs to detail the scope and interfaces of the process. More detailed 'desk top' procedures will also need to be produced. The typical contents of a Process Specification are:

- process name, description and administration – (version, Change control etc.)
- vision and mission statements
- scope, objectives and terms of reference
- process overview:
    - description and overview
    - inputs
    - sub processes
    - activities
    - outputs
    - triggers
    - tools and other deliverables
    - communication
- roles and responsibilities:
    - operational responsibilities
    - process owner
    - process members
    - process Users
    - other roles
- associated documentation
- interfaces:
    - to other SM processes
    - to other IT processes
    - to business processes
- dependencies:
    - on and to other SM processes
    - on and to other IT processes
    - on and to business processes
- formal targets:
    - measurements
    - metrics
    - targets and timescales

- reviews, assessment and audit
- reports produced by the process:
    - frequency
    - content
    - distribution
- glossary, acronyms and references.

APPENDIX G EXAMPLE COST-BENEFIT ANALYSIS FOR SERVICE MANAGEMENT PROCESSES

This Appendix is intended as an example of how to quantify the costs and benefits of implementing the processes described in ITIL. It is not intended to be comprehensive. Substitute the organisation's specific assumptions, purposes, costs, and benefits to get an example that is more suitable to the specific circumstances.

In this example, the following assumptions are made:

- all employees cost £50 an hour
- the organisation comprises 500 Users
- the total number of Incidents is 5,000 per year
- the average time to fix an Incident is 10 minutes
- a working year has 200 days.

Example costs and benefits are set out in Table G.1.

Process	Purpose	Cost Benefit Examples
Configuration Management	Controlling the IT infrastructure	As one of the benefits, following the implementation of Configuration Management, the Service Desk has a much greater insight into the relationship between Users, CIs and Incidents. The 3 people assigned to Incident matching can be reduced to 2, resulting in a benefit of 200*8*£50 = £80,000 a year.
	Ensuring that only authorised hardware and software is in use	
Incident Management	Continuity of the service levels	The implementation of Incident Management has resulted in a decrease in downtime per User; this is defined as the amount of time a User is on the phone to the Service Desk or cannot work because of a failure. If the downtime per User has gone down by 1 minute per person per day, this would save the organisation 1/60*500*200*£50 = £83,300 per year.
	Underpin Service Desk function	
Problem Management	Minimise disruption of the service level	Suppose that the implementation of Problem Management decreases the amount of recurring Incidents by 500 (10% of total) per year. This means a revenue of 500*10/60*£50 = > £4,000 per year.
Change Management	Efficient handling of Changes	Two Changes are implemented simultaneously, resulting in a major problem. The Customer support system fails, resulting in the loss of 50 Customers with an average purchasing power of £500. This has just cost the company £25,000.

Process	Purpose	Cost Benefit Examples
Release Management	Ensuring authorised software modules are used Provide means to build Change Releases Automating release of software	Suppose that a new software module is released containing a bug. The previous version should be reinstalled, but due to poor Version Management, the wrong version is used, resulting in a system shutdown that lasts for 3 hours and affects two thirds of all employees. This would cost the organisation 2/3x*500*£50*3 = £50,000.
Service Level Management	Agree on and control the service levels Understand business needs	Thanks to a clear set of agreements, the Service Desk is less troubled with calls that are not part of the services offered. This way the 4 Service Desk employees work 5% more efficiently, resulting in a gain of 4*5%*£500*8*200 = £16,000 a year.
Availability Management	Ensure high availability of services	Due to a physical error on a hard disk, a server supporting 100 people crashes. It takes 3 hours to have a new disk delivered and installed before starting up the system again. Costs: 100*3*£50 = £15,000. On a critical system, Availability Management processes would have highlighted the need for a mirror disk, which could automatically take over.
Capacity Management	Ensure the optimal use of IT	There is an over capacity of 20%. Assuming the IT infrastructure cost £5 million, it is possible to gain up to £1 million by implementing Capacity Management and frequently reassessing the necessary capacity.
IT Service Continuity Management	Ensure quick recovery after a disaster	A water pipe breaks, flooding the server room. It takes 2 days to be fully operational. The average User has missed 10 hours of work. Total costs (apart from the pumping): 500*10*£50 = £250,000. Please note that a good contingency plan doesn't come cheap; however the recovery costs (as in this example) could be dramatic – that is, if the organisation is still in business!
Financial Management	Provide insight, control and charge the costs of IT services	Imagine that the costs of IT services are charged to the departments that take them. A 10% reduction in the requests for new services would directly result in a 10% reduction of IT expenditure. The insight into the real costs in IT services proves to be surprising in practice; most Users do not have a clue about the costs.

Table G.1 – Example costs and benefits

APPENDIX H THE ITIL PROCESSES

H.1 Service Support

H.1.1 Configuration Management

Configuration Management covers the identification of all significant components within the IT Infrastructure and recording details of these components in the Configuration Management Database (CMDB). Importantly the Configuration Management system also records relationships between these components. It provides comprehensive information about all components in the infrastructure that enable all other processes to function more effectively and efficiently.

H.1.2 Change Management

Change Management covers the process of IT Change for all types of Change, from the Request for Change, to assessment, to scheduling, to implementing, and finally to the review. It is the Change Management process that produces approval (or otherwise), for any proposed Change.

H.1.3 Release Management

Release Management is very closely linked with Configuration Management and Change Management, and undertakes the planning, design, build, and testing of hardware and software to create a set of release components for a live environment. Activities cover the planning, preparation and scheduling of a release to Customers and locations.

H.1.4 Incident Management

The primary goal of the Incident Management process is to restore normal service as quickly as possible following loss of service, and to minimise the adverse impact on business operations, thus ensuring that the best possible levels of service quality and availability are maintained. An Incident is defined as any event which is not part of the standard operation of a service and which causes, or may cause, an interruption to, or a reduction in, the quality of that service.

H.1.5 Problem Management

The goal of Problem Management is to minimise the adverse impact of Incidents and Problems on the business that are caused by errors within the IT Infrastructure, and to prevent recurrence of Incidents related to these errors. In order to achieve this goal, Problem Management seeks to get to the root cause of Incidents and then initiate actions to improve or correct the situation. The Problem Management process has both reactive and proactive aspects. The reactive aspect is concerned with solving Problems in response to one or more Incidents. Proactive Problem Management is concerned with identifying and solving the underlying causes of Incident before they recur.

H.1.6   Service Desk

The Service Desk differs from the other main areas of Service Management in that it is not a process but is the central point of contact for Customers to report difficulties, complaints or questions. Additionally the Service Desk extends the range of services allowing business processes to be integrated into the Service Management infrastructure by providing an interface for other activities such as Customer Change requests, maintenance contracts, software licences, Service Level Agreements and Configuration Management.

Many Call Centres and Help Desks naturally evolve into Service Desks to improve and extend overall service to the Customers and the business.

H.2   Service Delivery

H.2.1   Service Level Management

Service Level Management is the processes of planning, coordinating, drafting, agreeing, monitoring and reporting on Service Level Agreements (SLAs), and the ongoing reviewing of service achievements to ensure that the required and cost justifiable service quality is maintained or where necessary improved. SLAs provide the basis for managing the relationship between the provider and the Customer.

H.2.2   Financial Management for IT Services

Financial Management is concerned with three main processes of Budgeting, IT Accounting and Charging. **Budgeting** is the process of predicting and controlling the spending of money within the enterprise and consists of a periodic negotiation cycle (usually annual) to set limits on budgets and the day to day monitoring of the current budgets. **IT Accounting** is the set of processes that enable the IT organisation fully to account for the way its money is spent – particularly the ability to identify costs by Customer, by service, by activity. **Charging** is the set of processes required to charge Customers for the services supplied to them. To achieve this requires sound Accounting, to a level of detail determined by the requirements of the analysis, billing and reporting processes.

H.2.3   Capacity Management

Capacity Management is the focal point for all IT performance and capacity issues. It is essential that Capacity Management has a close, two way relationship with the business strategy and planning processes within an organisation. The process needs to understand the long term strategy of the business while providing information on the latest ideas, trends and technologies being developed by the suppliers of computing hardware and software.

H.2.4   IT Service Continuity Management

IT Service Continuity Management is responsible for taking risk reduction measures to reduce the chances of major disasters occurring and for the production of an IT recovery plan which interfaces into the overall business continuity plans. The IT recovery plans will need to be cost effective and justified by the business.

H.2.5   Availability Management

Availability Management is concerned with the design, implementation, measurement and management of IT infrastructure availability to ensure the stated business requirements for availability are consistently met. Availability Management will consider all aspects of the IT infrastructure and supporting organisation which may impact availability, including training, skills, policy, process, procedures and tools.

APPENDIX I QUALITY

I.1 Quality Management

Quality Management for IT Services is a systematic way of ensuring that all the activities necessary to design, develop and implement IT services which satisfy the requirements of the organisation and of users take place as planned and that the activities are carried out cost-effectively.

The way that an organisation plans to manage its Operations so that it delivers quality services is specified by its Quality Management System. The Quality Management System defines the organisational structure, responsibilities, policies, procedures, processes, standards and resources required to deliver quality IT services. However, a Quality Management System will only function as intended if management and staff are committed to achieving its objectives.

This appendix gives brief details on a number of different Quality approaches – more detail on these and other approaches can be found on the Internet at www.dti.gov.uk/quality.

I.1.1 Deming

Quote

'We have learned to live in a world of mistakes and defective products as if they were necessary to life. It is time to adopt a new philosophy...'

(W. Edwards Deming, 1900-1993)

W. Edwards Deming is best known for his management philosophy for establishing quality, productivity, and competitive position. As part of this philosophy he formulated 14 points of attention for managers. Some of these points are more appropriate to Service Management than others.

For quality improvement Deming proposed the Deming Cycle or Circle. The four key stages are 'Plan, Do, Check, and Act' after which a phase of consolidation prevents the 'Circle' from 'rolling down the hill' as illustrated in Figure I.1.

The cycle is underpinned by a process led approach to management where defined processes are in place, the activities measured for compliance to expected values and outputs audited to validate and improve the process.

Example

Excerpts from Deming's 14 points relevant to Service Management

- break down barriers between departments (improves communications and management)

- management must learn their responsibilities, and take on leadership (process improvement requires commitment from the top; good leaders motivate people to improve themselves and therefore the image of the organisation)

- improve constantly (a central theme for service management is continual improvement; this is also a theme for Quality Management. A process led approach is key to achieve this target)

- institute a programme of education and self-improvement (learning and improving skills has been the focus of Service Management for many years)

- training on the job (linked to continual improvement)

- transformation is everyone's job (the emphasis being on teamwork and understanding).

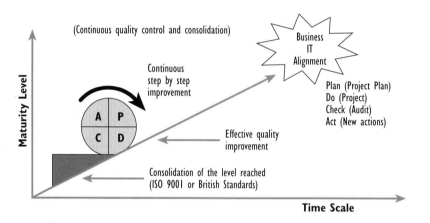

Figure I.1 – The Deming Cycle

I.1.2   Juran

Joseph Juran became a recognised name in the quality field in 1951 with the publication of the Quality Control Handbook. The appeal was to the Japanese initially, and Juran was asked to give a series of lectures in 1954 on planning, organisational issues, management responsibility for Quality, and the need to set goals and targets for improvement.

Juran devised a well-known chart, 'The Quality Trilogy', shown in Figure I.2, to represent the relationship between quality planning, quality control, and quality improvement on a project-by-project basis.

A further feature of Juran's approach is the recognition of the need to guide managers; this is achieved by the establishment of a quality council within an organisation, which is responsible for establishing processes, nominating projects, assigning teams, making improvements and providing the necessary resources.

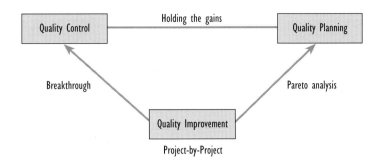

Figure I.2 – The Quality trilogy

Senior management plays a key role in serving on the quality council, approving strategic goals, allocating resources, and reviewing progress.

Juran promotes a four-phased approach to quality improvement, namely:

- Start-up – creating the necessary organisational structures and infrastructure
- Test – in which concepts are tried out in pilot programmes and results evaluated
- Scale-up – in which the basic concepts are extended based on positive feedback
- Institutionalisation – at which point quality improvements are linked to the strategic business plan.

I.1.3 Crosby

The Crosby TQM approach is very popular in the UK. However, despite its obvious success in the market, it has been subject to much criticism, primarily due to poor understanding, or a blinkered application of the approach in some organisations, using a limited definition of quality. The approach is based on Crosby's Four Absolutes of Quality Management, namely:

- Quality is conformance to requirement
- The system for causing quality is prevention and not appraisal
- The performance standard must be zero defects and not 'that's close enough'
- The measure of quality is the price of non-conformance and not indices.

The Crosby approach is often based on familiar slogans; however, organisations may experience difficulty in translating the quality messages into sustainable methods of quality improvement. Some organisations have found it difficult to integrate their quality initiatives, having placed their quality programme outside the mainstream management process.

Anecdotal evidence suggests that these pitfalls result in difficulties being experienced in sustaining active quality campaigns over a number of years in some organisations.

Crosby lacks the engineering rigour of Juran and significantly omits to design quality into the product or process, gearing the quality system towards a prevention-only policy. Furthermore, it fails to recognise that few organisations have appropriate management measures from which they can accurately ascertain the costs of non-conformance, and in some cases even the actual process costs!

I.1.4 Six Sigma

This is commonly described as a body of knowledge required to implement a generic quantitative approach to improvement. Six Sigma is a data-driven approach to analysing the root causes of problems and solving them. It is business output driven in relation to customer specification and focuses on dramatically reducing process variation using Statistical Process Control (SPC) measures. A process that operates at Six Sigma allows only 3.40 defects per million parts of output.

The Six Sigma approach has evolved from experience in manufacturing, and is therefore not readily applied to human processes and perhaps other processes that are not immediately apparent. The approach relies on trained personnel capable of identifying processes that need improvement and who can act accordingly. It does not contain a systematic approach for identifying improvement opportunities or facilitate with prioritisation.

Six Sigma perhaps offers another path toward measurable improvement for CMM Level 3 organisations, but this alone may make it difficult to apply in the context of Service Management compared to software engineering.

There are research reservations on applying validation and measurement to process improvement and particularly in the application of SPC to non-manufacturing engineering processes. It has been found that a Goal, Question, Metric (GQM) approach provides suitable measures, rather than a statistical method. It is still somewhat a controversial area, and even the SW-CMM at the higher levels (4–5) has come in for some academic criticism in this area. However, there are indications that Six Sigma is being applied in the service sector and, with good Service Management support tools, tracking of incidents, etc., would allow this approach to be used for process improvement.

I.2 Formal quality initiatives

I.2.1 Quality standards

International Standards Organisation ISO 9000

An important set of International Standards for Quality Assurance is the ISO 9000 range, a set of five universal standards for a Quality Assurance system that is accepted around the world. At the turn of the millennium, 90 or so countries have adopted ISO 9000 as the cornerstone of their national standards. When a product or service is purchased from a company that is registered to the appropriate ISO 9000 standard, the purchaser has important assurances that the quality of what they will receive will be as expected.

The most comprehensive of the standards is ISO 9001. It applies to industries involved in the design, development, manufacturing, installation and servicing of products or services. The standards apply uniformly to companies in any industry and of any size.

The BSI Management Overview of IT Service Management is a modern update of the original document PD0005, which was published in 1995. The Management Overview is a management level introduction to Service Management, and in fact can be used as an introduction to ITIL . This is also now supported by a formal standard, BS 15000 (Specification for IT Service Management). ITIL is in many countries the *de facto* standard, and with the help of BSI and ISO, it is hoped that a formal international standard based on ITIL will soon be in place. The BSI Standard and Management Overview cover the established ITIL Service Support and Service Delivery processes, as well as some additional topics such as implementing the processes.

I.2.2 Total Quality Systems: EFQM

Quote

'...the battle for Quality is one of the prerequisites for the success of your companies and for our collective success.'

(Jacques Delors, president of the Europeam Commission, at the signing of the letter of intent in Brussels to establish EFQM on 15 September 1988.)

The EFQM Excellence Model

The European Foundation for Quality Management (EFQM) was founded in 1988 by the Presidents of 14 major European companies, with the endorsement of the European Commission. The present membership is in excess of 600 very well-respected organisations, ranging from major multinationals and important national companies to research institutes in prominent European universities.

EFQM provides an excellent model for those wishing to achieve business excellence in a programme of continual improvement.

EFQM mission statement

The mission statement is:

> **To stimulate and assist organisations throughout Europe to participate in improvement activities leading ultimately to excellence in customer satisfaction, employee satisfaction, impact on society and business results; and to support the Managers of European organisations in accelerating the process of making Total Quality Management a decisive factor for achieving global competitive advantage.**

Depiction of the EFQM Excellence Model

The EFQM Excellence Model consists of 9 criteria and 32 sub-criteria; it is illustrated in Figure I.3.

In the model there is explicit focus on the value to users of the 'Plan, Do, Check, Act' cycle to business operations (see Section I.1.1), and the need to relate everything that is done, and the measurements taken, to the goals of business policy and strategy.

Self-assessment and maturity: the EFQM maturity scale

One of the tools provided by EFQM is the self-assessment questionnaire. The self-assessment process allows the organisation to discern clearly its strengths and also any areas where improvements can be made. The questionnaire process culminates in planned improvement actions, which are then monitored for progress.

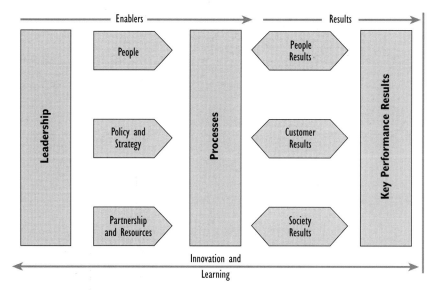

©EFQM. The EFQM excellence Model is a registered trademark

Figure I.3 – The EFQM Excellence Model

In this assessment progress can be checked against a five-point maturity scale:

1   Product orientation

2   Process orientation (the maturity stage aimed for by the original ITIL)

3   System orientation (the maturity target for ITIL-compliant organisations in the new millennium)

4   Chain orientation

5   Total quality.

I.2.3   Quality awards

To demonstrate a successful adaptation of the EFQM model, some companies aim for the European Quality Award, a process that allows Europe to recognise its most successful organisations and promote them as role models of excellence for others to copy.

The US equivalent to this award is the Malcolm Baldridge Quality Award for Quality Management. The Malcolm Baldridge National Quality Improvement Act of 1987 established an annual US National Quality Award. The purpose of the Award was (and still is) to promote awareness of quality excellence, to recognise quality achievements of US companies, and to publicise successful quality strategies.

For the Malcolm Baldridge Award, there are three categories:

■   Manufacturing companies or sub-units

■   Service companies or sub-units

■   Small businesses.

The criteria against which firms are judged are:

1   Leadership

2   Strategic planning

3 Customer and market focus

4 Information and analysis

5 Human resource development and management

6 Process management

7 Business results.

For the European Quality Award, there are four possible categories:

- Companies
- Operational units of companies
- Public sector organisations
- Small and medium enterprises.

The criteria against which candidate organisations are measured are:

1 Leadership

2 People

3 Policy and strategy

4 Partnerships and resources

5 Processes

6 People results

7 Customer results

8 Society results

9 Key performance results.

In the EFQM Excellence Model the first four criteria are defined as enablers. Best practice in ITIL process implementations show that placing proper emphasis on these topics increases the chances for success. The key points for the four enablers are listed below.

Leadership

- Organise a kick-off session involving everyone
- Be a role model
- Encourage and support the staff.

People management

- Create awareness
- Recruit new staff and/or hire temporary staff to prevent Service Levels being affected during implementation stages
- Develop people through training and experience
- Align human resource plans with policy and strategy
- Adopt a coaching style of management
- Align performance with salaries.

Policy and strategy

- Communicate mission, vision and values
- Align communication plans with the implementation stages.

Partnerships and resources

- Establish partnerships with subcontractors and customers
- Use financial resources in support of policy and strategy
- Utilise existing assets.

APPENDIX J THE PROCESS MATURITY FRAMEWORK (PMF)

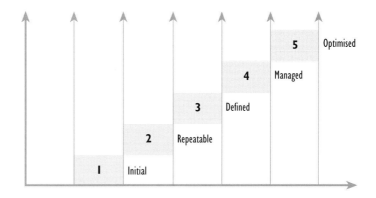

Figure J.1 – IT Organisation Growth Model

The PMF can be used either as a framework to assess the maturity of each of the ten Service Management processes individually, or to measure the maturity of the overall Service Management process as a whole. This is an approach that has been widely used in the IT industry for a number of years, with many proprietary models being used by a number of organisations. This particular PMF has been developed to bring a common, best practice approach to the review and assessment of Service Management process maturity. This framework can be used by organisations to internally review their own Service Management processes as well as third party organisations brought in as external assessors/auditors.

The use of the PMF in the assessment of Service Management processes relies on an appreciation of the IT Organisation Growth Model (Figure J.1). The maturity of the Service Management processes is heavily dependent upon the stage of growth of the IT organisation as a whole. It is difficult, if not impossible, to develop the maturity of the Service Management processes beyond the maturity and capability of the overall IT organisation. The maturity of the IT organisation is not just dependent upon the maturity of the Service Management processes. Each level requires a change of a combination of elements in order to be fully effective. Therefore a review of processes will require an assessment to be completed against the five areas of:

1 Vision and steering

2 Process

3 People

4 Technology

5 Culture.

These are the five areas contained within the framework for change contained in Section 3.2.

The major characteristics of each level of the PMF are as follows:

Initial (Level 1): The process has been recognised but there is little or no process management activity and it is allocated no importance, resources or focus within the organisation. This level can also be described as 'ad hoc' or occasionally even 'chaotic'.

Vision and steering	Minimal funds and resources with little activity
	Results temporary, not retained
	Sporadic reports and reviews
Process	Loosely defined processes and procedures, used reactively when problems occur
	Totally reactive processes
	Irregular, unplanned activities
People	Loosely defined roles or responsibilities
Technology	Manual processes or a few specific discrete tools (pockets/islands)
Culture	Tool and technology based and driven with a strong activity focus

Table J.1 – Initial (Level 1)

Repeatable (Level 2): The process has been recognised and is allocated little importance, resource or focus within the operation. Generally activities related to the process are uncoordinated, irregular, without direction and are directed towards process effectiveness.

Vision and steering	No clear objectives or formal targets
	Funds and resources available
	Irregular, unplanned activities, reporting and reviews
Process	Defined processes and procedures
	Largely reactive process
	Irregular, unplanned activities
People	Self contained roles and responsibilities
Technology	Many discrete tools, but a lack of control
	Data stored in separate locations
Culture	Product and service based and driven

Table J.2 – Repeatable (Level 2)

Defined (Level 3): The process has been recognised and is documented but there is no formal agreement, acceptance and recognition of its role within the IT operation as a whole. However the process has a process owner, formal objectives and targets with allocated resources and is focused on the efficiency as well as the effectiveness of the process. Reports and results are stored for future reference.

Vision and steering	Documented and agreed formal objectives and targets
	Formally published, monitored and reviewed plans
	Well funded and appropriately resourced
	Regular, planned reporting and reviews
Process	Clearly defined and well publicised processes and procedures
	Regular, planned activities
	Good documentation
	Occasionally proactive process
People	Clearly defined and agreed roles and responsibilities
	Formal objectives and targets
	Formalised process training plans
Technology	Continuous data collection with alarm and threshold monitoring
	Consolidated data retained and used for formal planning, forecasting and trending
Culture	Service and Customer oriented with a formalised approach

Table J.3 – Defined (Level 3)

Managed (Level 4): The process has now been fully recognised and accepted throughout IT. It is service focused and has objectives and targets that are based on business objectives and goals. The process is fully defined, managed and has become proactive, with documented, established interfaces and dependencies with other IT process.

Vision and steering	Clear direction with business goals, objectives and formal targets, measured progress
	Effective management reports actively used
	Integrated process plans linked to business and IT plans
	Regular improvements, planned and reviewed
Process	Well defined processes, procedures and standards, included in all IT staff job descriptions
	Clearly defined process interfaces and dependencies
	Integrated Service Management and systems development processes
	Mainly proactive process
People	Inter and intra process team working
	Responsibilities clearly defined in all IT job descriptions

Technology	Continuous monitoring measurement, reporting and threshold alerting to a centralised set of integrated toolsets, databases and processes
Culture	Business focused with an understanding of the wider issues

Table J.4 – Managed (Level 4)

Optimising (Level 5): The process has now been fully recognised and has strategic objectives and goals aligned with overall strategic business and IT goals. These have now become 'institutionalised' as part of the everyday activity for everyone involved with the process. A self contained continuous process of improvement is established as part of the process, which is now developing a pre emptive capability.

Vision and steering	Integrated strategic plans inextricably linked with overall business plans, goals and objectives
	Continuous, monitoring, measurement, reporting alerting and reviews linked to a continuous process of improvement
	Regular reviews and/or audits for effectiveness, efficiency and compliance
Process	Well defined processes and procedures part of corporate culture
	Proactive and pre emptive process
People	Business aligned objectives and formal targets actively monitored as part of the everyday activity
	Roles and responsibilities part of an overall corporate culture
Technology	Well documented overall tool architecture with complete integration in all areas of people, processes and technology
Culture	A continuous improvement attitude, together with a strategic business focus.
	An understanding of the value of IT to the business and its role within the business value chain

Table J.5 – Optimising (Level 5)

APPENDIX K EXAMPLE OF A STAKEHOLDER MAP

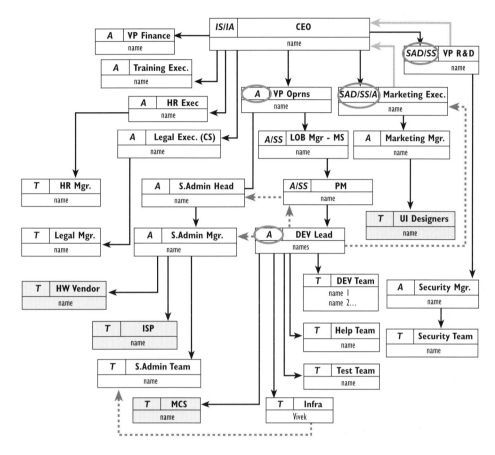

Figure K.1 – Role map diagram

Figure K.1 provides an example of a stakeholder map and Figure K.2 explains the legends used in the stakeholder map. Some important notes:

- all Advocates, Sponsors and Agents are also Targets
- the greyed boxes are external Players – all external players are by default Targets
- sequence of roles reads left to right (e.g., this person acts first as an initiating advocate to gain the sponsorship necessary to proceed; he or she then serves as an agent to facilitate implementation)
- the following mappings have been done:
  - IA and SA map to Change Advocate *(AD)* – a person who actively supports the Change
  - IS and SS map to Change Sponsor *(S)* – a person sponsoring the Change
  - A maps to Change Agent *(A)* – a person who actively leads the change within their workgroup
    T maps to Change Recipient (T) – a person whose work is directly affected by the change.

IS	Initiating Sponsor — an individual or group who has the ultimate responsibility to legitimise a change. The initiating sponsor has the power to engage the Change for everyone below.
SS	Sustaining Sponsor — an individual or group who ensures that the initiating sponsor's directives are implemented on time and within budget in his or her respective area. This person sustains the Change to everyone below and may also serve as a target and/or agent to his or her sponsor above.
A	Agent — an individual or group responsible for developing and carrying out implementation plans. The agent reports, for purposes of implementing the Change to a particular sponsor.
T	Target — an individual or group who must change. (All sponsors, agents, and advocates are automatically viewed as targets, and it it not necessary to list the 'T' when labelling their role designation.)
IA	Initiating Advocate — an individual or group who originally presents an idea for change with the intent of gaining legitimisation support from a sponsor. The initiating advocate may be located anywhere in the organisation and may, once the Change is sponsored, become a sustaining sponsor, agent, and target, during implementation.
SA	Sustaining Advocate — an individual or group who helps maintain sponsor commitment for a Change. The sustaining advocate may also be located anywhere in the organisation.
⟶	Sponsor Influence: the sponsor sanctions the Change for the person indicated by the arrow.
⟶	Advocate Influence: the advocate influences the person indicated by the arrow.
┄┄➤	Agent Assistance: the agent assists the person indicated by the arrow.
⬭	Once all the key roles in a Role Map diagram are identified, it is usually apparent that certain individuals or groups represent critical junctures, or 'gates'. These are identified by an oval, drawn around the designation. If these vital people are not committed to the Change or are not sufficiently prepared to perform their roles, the entire component's success could be in jeopardy. Conversely, when these key 'gates' represent people who are highly committed and skilled, the likelihood for success is enhanced.

Figure K.2 – Role Map Diagram legends

Note that the mappings are with respect to the terminology used in the Role Map Application tool (IA, SA, IS, SS, A and T), which have been used so far in the document above – especially the Role Map Diagram.

#	SMART Title	Org. Title	Name	S	AD	A	T	Comments
1	Business Operations Executive	CEO	Put a name here	●	●			The PROPONENT of the initiative.
2	Research and Development Executive	VP R&D	Put a name here	●	●		●	
3	Research and Development Manager	Security Team Mgr.	Put a name here			●	●	
4	Research and Development Staff	Security Team	Put a name here				●	
5	Business Operations Manager	VP Oprns.	Put a name here			●	●	
6	IT System Administration Executive	S.Admin Exec.	Put a name here			●	●	Create New role.
7	IT System Administration Manager	S.Admin Mgr.	Put a name here			●	●	Create New role.
8	IT System Administration Staff	S.Admin Team.	Put a name here				●	Create New role.
9	Third Party Hard Ware Vendor	HW Vendor	Put a name here				●	Create New role.
10	Third Party Service Provider - ISP	ISP	Put a name here				●	Create New role.
11	Information Technology Executive	LOB Mgr. - MS	Put a name here	●		●	●	
12	Information technology Manager	PM	Put a name here	●		●	●	
13	Information technology Manager	Dev. Lead	Put a name here			●	●	
14	Information technology Staff	Dev. Team	Put a name here				●	
15			Put a name here				●	
16			Put a name here				●	
17			Put a name here				●	
18		Test Team	Put a name here				●	
19		Help Team	Put a name here				●	
20		Infra.	Put a name here				●	
21	Third Party Service Provider - IT Consultant	MCS	Put a name here				●	Create New role.
22	Legal Executive	Legal Exec. (CS)	Put a name here			●	●	
23	Legal Manager	Legal Mgr.	Put a name here				●	
24	Human Resources Executive	HR Exec.	Put a name here			●	●	
25	Human Resources Manager	HR Mgr.	Put a name here				●	
26	Training Executive	Training Exec.	Put a name here			●	●	
27	Sales and Marketing Executive	Marketing Exec.	Put a name here	●		●	●	
28	Sales and Marketing Manager	Marketing Mgr.	Put a name here			●	●	
29	Finance Executive	VP Finance.	Put a name here			●	●	

Key: SMART (Specific, Measurable, Achievable, Realistic and Time related)

AD (Change Advocate)

S (Change Sponsor)

A (Change Agent)

T (Change Recipient)

Figure K.3 – Stakeholder map

APPENDIX L USE OF TOOLS

Software tools should be capable of underpinning the IT Service Management processes. One of the main objectives of the Service Management framework is the administration of information used to manage the quality and optimisation of IT services. As a rule, a tool should support 100% of the mandatory functional requirements and 80% of desired functional requirements.

Software tools should increase efficiency and effectiveness, and provide a wealth of management information leading to the identification of weak areas. The longer term benefits to be gained are cost savings and increased productivity, which in turn can lead to an increase in the quality of the IT service provision.

The use of tools will enable the centralisation of key processes and the automation of core Service Management processes. The raw data collected in the databases can be analysed, resulting in the identification of 'trends'. Preventative measures can then be implemented again increasing the quality of the IT service provision.

The following is a sample list of best practice requirements that organisations should consider when evaluating the functional abilities of a Service Management tool:

- a careful evaluation of tool requirements has been performed before selection
- all the mandatory and desirable functional tool requirements are based on a defined IT process
  - all mandatory requirements covered
  - the tool provides a minimum of eighty per cent compliance for all operational requirements
  - the tool does not require extensive product customisation
  - the tool supports the ITIL processes
  - the tool satisfies current and future business requirements
- the tool provides the required interfaces with Systems Management tools
- the tool provides the required interfaces with business processes such as HR, financial, and research and development.

L.1 Other points for consideration

Some points that organisations should consider when evaluating the functionality of a Service Management tool:

- data structure, data handling and integration
- integration of multi vendor infrastructure components, and the need to absorb new components in the future – these will place particular demands on the data handling and modelling capabilities of the tool
- conformity to international open standards
- flexibility in implementation, usage and data sharing
- usability – the ease of use permitted by the User interface
- support for monitoring service levels – response and resolution

- distributed clients with a centralised shared database (e.g. client server)

- conversion requirements for previously tracked data

- data back up, control and security

- support options provided by the tool vendor

- organisational constraints:
    - impact on the organisation
    - staff availability, experience and skill sets

- implementation complexity (synergistic risk)

- costs:
    - software/hardware (purchase and installation)
    - licenses/training/development and customisation
    - consulting.

L.2 Practical guidelines for the selection of IT Service Management tools

Consideration must be given to the exact requirements for the tool. What are the mandatory requirements and what are the desired requirements? Some practical guidelines:

- The tool must support the processes; don't modify processes to fit the tool. Where possible it is better to purchase a fully integrated tool to underpin many (if not all) Service Management processes. If this is not possible, consideration must be given to the interfaces between the various tools.

- It is essential to have Statement Of Requirements (SOR) for use during the selection process; this statement can be used as a 'tick list'. The requirements should be separated into 'should haves' or mandatory requirements and 'nice to haves' or desirable requirements.

- The tool must be adequately flexible to support your required access rights. You must be able to determine who is permitted to access what data and for what purpose, e.g. read access to Customers.

- In the early stages consideration must also be given to the platform on which the tool will be expected to operate – this may be on existing hardware and software or a new purchase. There may be restrictions laid down by IT Strategy – for example, all new products may have to reside on specific Servers. This would restrict which products that could be included in the evaluation process.

- Make sure that the procurement fit within existing approved budgets.

- There are many Service Management tools available. Don't stick to the one(s) the organisation knows about. Surf the Web (for instance tools2manage it.com), look at Service Management publications, ask other organisations, ask consultants or talk to the *it*SMF to see what products are available. There may be a User Group for the product – if there is, talk to the Chairperson; this may lead to useful feedback.

- During the early stages of the vetting process think about vendor and tool credibility. Are they still going to be supporting the purchase in a few months' or a year's time? Consider the past record of the supplier as well as that of the tool. Telephone the supplier Service desk to see how easy it is to get through, and ask some test questions to assess technical competence.

■ Ask the vendor to arrange a visit to a reference site to see what the experience is with tool in practice – if possible without the vendor or supplier present. Make sure that the organisation has similar requirements of the tool. See the tool in operation and speak to the Users about their experiences, both initially and ongoing.

■ Don't limit your requirements to functionality, ask about the product's ability to perform, enlarge the size of the databases, recover from failure, and maintain data integrity. Does the product conform to international standards? Is it efficient enough to enable you to meet your Service Level Requirements?

■ Assess the management reports generated by the tool. In some tools, the generation of meaningful reports can be a cumbersome and time consuming task. To monitor the output of the processes the tool should have many ways of aggregating the data in meaningful and, for the business, understandable, ways.

■ Assess the training needs of the organisation and evaluate the capability of the supplier to provide the appropriate training. In particular, consider training costs, training location, time required, how soon after training the tool will be in use. During the implementation process ensure that sufficient training is provided – think about how the new tool will impact both IT and Customer.

■ Also ensure that interfaces with other tools and telephony are functioning correctly. It is wise to identify whether the planned combination has been used (or tried) elsewhere, and with what results. Consider parallel running before finally going live.

A much more detailed evaluation must now be completed. Demonstrations of the products need to be arranged. Ensure that all the relevant members of staff are involved. Be wary of demonstrations; always see the live product in operation. If possible, provide the test data and assess the provided results against expectations. Be cautious of being promised things in the next release. Use a reference site to confirm impressions from the demonstration. Use the SOR and adjust the 'tick list' during the demonstrations of the products. Refer to this later to assist in reducing the shortlist to the final chosen product.

It obviously doesn't end when the product has been selected. In many ways this could be considered as only the beginning. The tool now has to be implemented. Once the hardware platform has been prepared and the software loaded, data population needs to be considered. What, where from, how and when? Timing is important to the implementation, testing and finally going live processes. Resources must be available to ensure success. In other words, don't schedule during a known busy period, such as year-end processing.

Following live implementation, hold regular meetings with both IT and Customers to ensure the agreed benefits have been realised. Some aspects may have to be refined. During this process also consider the performance of the supplier. If they have not performed to your expectations, they should be advised (in writing) as soon as possible.

INDEX

Other Information Sources and Services

The IT Service Management Forum (itSMF)

The IT Service Management Forum Ltd (itSMF) is the only internationally recognised and independent body dedicated to IT Service Management. It is a not-for-profit organisation, wholly owned, and principally operated, by its membership.

The itSMF is a major influence on, and contributor to, Industry Best Practice and Standards worldwide, working in partnership with OGC (the owners of ITIL), the British Standards Institution (BSI), the Information Systems Examination Board (ISEB) and the Examination Institute of the Netherlands (EXIN).

Founded in the UK in 1991, there are now a number of chapters around the world with new ones seeking to join all the time. There are well in excess of 1000 organisations covering over 10,000 individuals represented in the membership. Organisations range from large multi-nationals such as AXA, GuinnessUDV, HP, Microsoft and Procter & Gamble in all market sectors, through central & local bodies, to independent consultants.

How to contact us:

The IT Service Management Forum Ltd
Webbs Court
8 Holmes Road
Earley
Reading RG6 7BH
Tel: +44 (0) 118 926 0888
Fax: +44 (0) 118 926 3073
Email: service@itsmf.com
or visit our web-site at:
www.itsmf.com

ITIL training and professional qualifications

There are currently two examining bodies offering equivalent qualifications: ISEB (The Information Systems Examining Board), part of the British Computer Society, and Stitching EXIN (The Netherlands Examinations Institute). Jointly with OGC and itSMF (the IT Service Management Forum), they work to ensure that a common standard is adopted for qualifications worldwide. The syllabus is based on the core elements of ITIL and complies with ISO9001 Quality Standard. Both ISEB and EXIN also accredit training organisations to deliver programmes leading to qualifications.

For further information:

visit ISEB's web-site at:
www.bcs.org.uk

and EXIN:
www.exin.nl

Best Practice:
the OGC approach with ITIL® and PRINCE®

OGC Best Practice is an approach to management challenges as well as the application of techniques and actions.

Practical, flexible and adaptable, management guidance from OGC translates the very best of the world's practices into guidance of an internationally recognised standard. Both PRINCE2 and ITIL publications can help every organisation to:

- Run projects more efficiently
- Reduce project risk
- Purchase IT more cost effectively
- Improve organisational Service Delivery.

What is ITIL and why use it?

ITIL's starting point is that organisations do not simply use IT; they depend on it. Managing IT as effectively as possible must therefore be a high priority.

ITIL consists of a unique library of guidance on providing quality IT services. It focuses tightly on the customer, cost effectiveness and building a culture that puts the emphasis on IT performance.

Used by hundreds of the world's most successful organisations, its core titles are available in print, Online Subscription and CD-ROM formats. They are:

- Service Support
- Service Delivery
- Planning to Implement Service Management
- Application Management
- ICT Infrastructure Management
- Security Management
- The Business Perspective Volume 1 and 2
- Software Asset Management

What is PRINCE2 and why use it?

Since its introduction in 1989, PRINCE has been widely adopted by both the public and private sectors and is now recognised as a de facto standard for project management – and for the management of change.

PRINCE2, the most evolved version, is driven by its experts and users to offer control, transparency, focus and ultimate success for any project you need to implement.

Publications are available in various formats: print, Online Subscription and CD-ROM. Its main titles are:

- Managing Successful Projects with PRINCE2
- People Issues and PRINCE2
- PRINCE2 Pocket Book
- Tailoring PRINCE2
- Business Benefits through Project Management

Other related titles:
- Passing the PRINCE2 Examinations
- Managing Successful Programmes
- Management of Risk – Guidance for Practitioners
- Buying Software – A best practice approach

Ordering

The full range of ITIL and PRINCE2 publications can be purchased direct via **www.get-best-practice.co.uk** or through calling TSO Customer Services on **0870 600 5522**. If you are outside of the UK please contact your local agent, for details email **sales@tso.co.uk** For information on Network Licenses for CD-ROM and Online Subscription please email **network.sales@tso.co.uk**

You are also able to subscribe to content online through this website or by calling TSO Customer Services on **0870 600 5522**. For more information on how to subscribe online please refer to our help pages on the website.

Dear customer ■ ■ ■ ■ ■ ■ ■ ■ ■ ■ ■ ■ ■ ▪ ▫ ▫

We would like to hear from you with any comments or suggestions that you have on how we can improve our current products or develop new ones for the ITIL series. Please complete this questionnaire and we will enter you into our quarterly draw. The winner will receive a copy of Software Asset Management worth £35!

1 Personal Details

Name ....

Organisation ....

Job Title ....

Department ....

Address ....

....

Postcode ....

Telephone Number ....

Email ....

2 Nature of Organisation (tick one box only)

☐ Consultancy/Training
☐ Computing/IT/Software
☐ Industrial
☐ Central Government
☐ Local Government
☐ Academic/Further education
☐ Private Health
☐ Public Health (NHS)
☐ Finance
☐ Construction
☐ Telecommunications
☐ Utilities
☐ Other (Please specify)

....

3 How did you hear about ITIL?

☐ Work/Colleagues
☐ Internet/Web (please specify)

....

☐ Marketing Literature
☐ itSMF
☐ Other (please specify)

....

4 Where did you purchase this book?

☐ Web – www.tso.co.uk/bookshop
☐ Web – www.get-best-practice.co.uk
☐ Web – Other (please specify)

....

☐ Bookshop (please specify)

....

☐ Training Course
☐ Other (please specify)

....

5 How many people use ITIL in your company?

☐ 1-5
☐ 6-10
☐ 11-50
☐ 51-200
☐ 201+

6 How many people use your copy of this title?

☐ 0
☐ 1-5
☐ 6-10
☐ 11+

7 Overall, how do you rate this title?

☐ Excellent
☐ Very Good
☐ Good
☐ Fair
☐ Poor

8 What do you most like about the book? (tick all that apply)

☐ Ease of use
☐ Well structured
☐ Contents
☐ Index
☐ Hints and tips
☐ Other (Please specify)

....

9 Do you have any suggestions for improvement?

....

....

....

....

10 How do you use this book? (tick all that apply)

☐ Problem Solver
☐ Reference
☐ Tutorial
☐ Other (please specify)

....

[PTO]

11 Did you know there are 7 core titles in the **ITIL** series?

☐ No
☐ Yes

12 Do you have any other **ITIL** titles?

☐ No
☐ Yes (please specify)

....

13 Do you use the **ITIL** CDs?

☐ No
☐ Yes (please specify)

....

14 Are you aware that most of the **ITIL** series is now available as online content at **www.get-best-practice.co.uk?**

☐ Yes
☐ No

15 Do you currently subscribe to any online content found at **www.get-best-practice.co.uk?**

☐ No
☐ Yes (please specify)

....

16 Did you know that you can network your CDs and Online Subscription, to offer your project managers access to this material at their desktop?

Yes/No

☐ Please tick this box if you require further information.

17 Did you know that you are able to purchase a maintenance agreement for your CD-ROM that will allow you to receive immediately any revised versions, at no additional cost?

Yes/No

☐ Please tick this box if you require further information.

18 What business change guidance/methods does your company use?

☐ PRINCE2
☐ Managing Successful Programmes
☐ Management of Risk
☐ Successful Delivery Toolkit
☐ Business Systems Development (BSD)
☐ Other (please specify)

....

19 What is the job title of the person who makes the decision to implement **ITIL** and/or purchase IT?

....

....

20 Which three websites do you visit the most?

1 ....

2 ....

3 ....

21 Which 3 professional magazines do you read the most?

1 ....

2 ....

3 ....

22 Will you be attending any events or conferences this year related to IT, if so, which?

....

To enter your Questionnaire into our monthly draw please return this form to our Freepost Address:

Marketing – ITIL Questionnaire
TSO
Freepost ANG4748
Norwich
NR3 1YX

The ITIL series is available in a range of formats: hard copy, CD-ROM and now available as an Online Subscription. For further details and to purchase visit **www.get-best-practice.co.uk**

Any further enquiries or questions about ITIL or the Office of Government Commerce should be directed to the OGC Service Desk:

The OGC Service Desk
Rosebery Court
St Andrews Business Park
Norwich
NR7 0HS

Email: ServiceDesk@ogc.gsi.gov.uk
Telephone: 0845 000 4999

TSO will not sell, rent or pass any of your details onto interested third parties. The details you supply will be used for market research purposes only and to keep you up to date with TSO products and services which we feel maybe of interest to you. **If you would like us to use your information to keep you updated please indicate how you would like us to communicate with you:**

Telephone ☐   **Email** ☐   **Mail** ☐